KU-327-568

CONTENTS

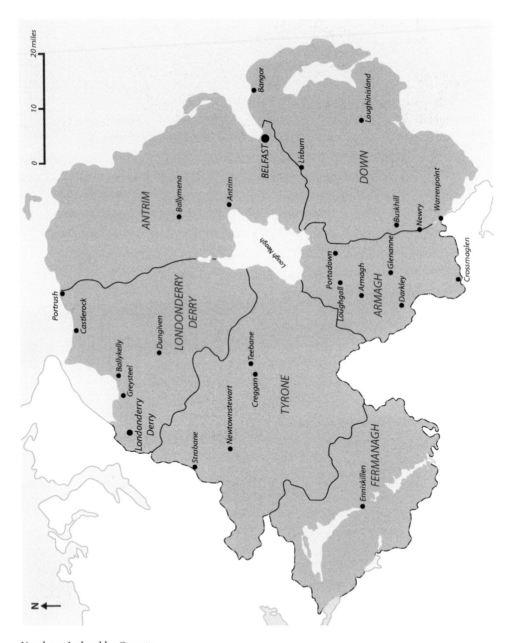

Northern Ireland by County

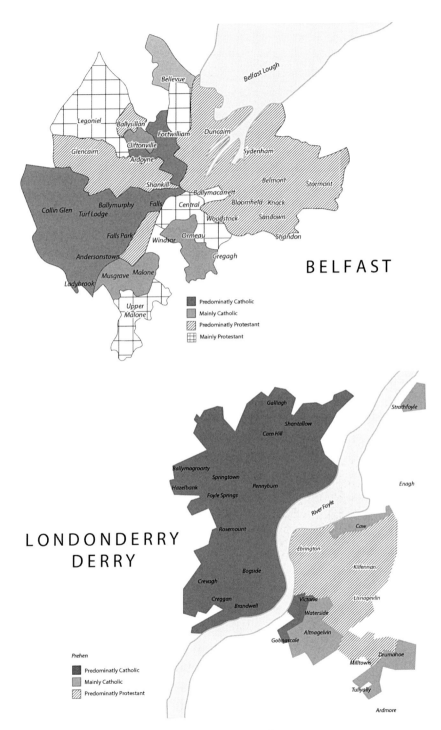

Belfast & Londonderry / Derry: Religious Demographics

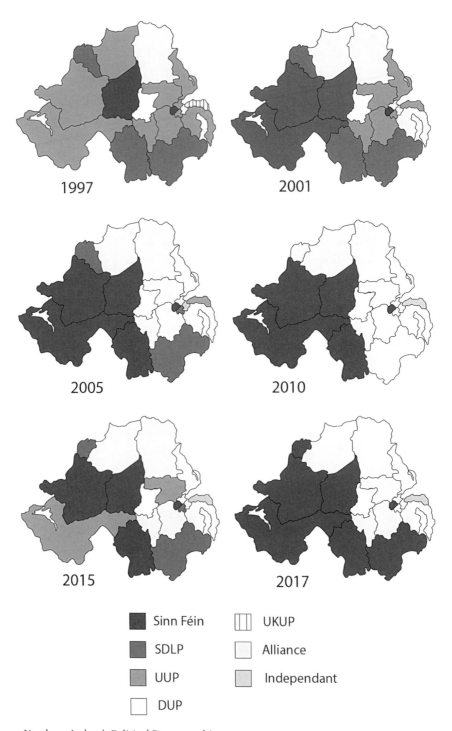

1997

2001

2005

2010

2015

2017

	Sinn Féin	⦀	UKUP
	SDLP		Alliance
	UUP		Independant
	DUP		

Northern Ireland: Political Demographics 1997–2017

GLOSSARY OF TERMS

14 Int	14 Field Security & Intelligence Company
CAIN	Conflict Archive on the Internet
Det	14 Field Security & Intelligence Company
DUP	Democratic Unionist Party (also UDUP, Ulster DUP)
FRU	Force Research Unit
GFA	Good Friday Agreement
GPMG	general-purpose machine gun (normally the FN 7.62 MAG)
INLA	Irish National Liberation Army
IPLO	Irish People's Liberation Organization
IRA	Irish Republican Army
LVF	Loyalist Volunteer Force
MO	modus operandi
MRF	Military Reaction Force
NICRA	Northern Ireland Civil Rights Association
OIRA	Official Irish Republican Army
OO	Orange Order
OSF	Official Sinn Féin
OV	Orange Volunteers (also RHD)
OUP	Official Unionist Party (also UUP)
PAF	Protestant Action Force
PAG	Protestant Action Group
PIRA	Provisional IRA
PSF	Provisional Sinn Féin
PSNI	Police Service of Northern Ireland
RHC	Red Hand Commando (also UVF)
RHD	Red Hand Defenders
RIR	Royal Irish Rangers
RTÉ	Raidió Teilifís Éireann, the national public service broadcaster of the Republic of Ireland
RUC	Royal Ulster Constabulary
SAS	22 Special Air Service
SB	Special Branch (of the RUC)
SDLP	Social Democratic & Labour Party

SDP	Social Democratic Party
SF	Sinn Féin
SRU	Special Reconnaissance Unit, 14 Int
TA	Territorial Army
UDA	Ulster Defence Association
UDR	Ulster Defence Regiment
UFF	Ulster Freedom Fighters (UDA)
ULA	Ulster Loyalist Association
USC	Ulster Special Constabulary (B Specials)
UUP	Ulster Unionist Party
UVF	Ulster Volunteer Force

PREAMBLE

How Did it Come to This?

It is, of course, no secret that undercover special forces and intelligence agencies operated covertly in Northern Ireland and the Irish Republic throughout the 'troubles' from 1969 to 1999, and beyond. What is less well known is how these units were recruited, how they operated, their strategy and mission and what they actually did. This book provides a record of their murders, torture, collusion, shooting to kill, undercover conflict, covert surveillance, reconnaissance and intelligence-gathering.

An astonishing number of clandestine agencies were active in the province during The Troubles: this account focuses on the Official IRA and the Provisional IRA, INLA, Military Reaction Force (MRF) and the Special Reconnaissance Unit, also known as the 14 Field Security & Intelligence Company ('The Det') and the SAS; it also deals with the operations and functions of RUC Special Branch, the UDR, the UDA, the UVF and the less well-known but equally lethal Red Hand Commando, the Glenanne Gang, the Loyalist Volunteer Force (LVF) and the Red Hand Defenders. The Force Research Unit (FRU) and MI5 are also covered.

The book explores such still contentious and challenging issues as shoot-to-kill, murder squads, the 'Disappeared', political assassinations and British government collusion with loyalists. Operations such as Loughgall and the Gibraltar Operation Flavius are examined. Official, hitherto classified papers newly released by the Irish government in December 2017 are assessed.

The glue that joins all this together is the prevalence of 'murder squads' during The Troubles, the title of the series of which this volume is part. The various agencies operating in The Troubles have the dubious distinction of rubbing shoulders with other murder squads and their atrocities that have tainted world history down the years. The intention, the aims and scope of *The Troubles* is certainly not to publish (yet another) melodramatic or sensationalist, unsubstantiated and gratuitous account. Rather, the book is intended to give an objective, non-partisan, non-judgemental description of the serial killing and murderous activity that afflicted Northern Ireland from 1969—to let the facts, as far as they have been allowed to emerge, speak for themselves, In addition, it is an attempt to correct the imbalance in various accounts of various events caused largely by the systematic and overt suppression of pertinent facts, by British government collusion and by the false facts pedalled by successive governments in relation to government policy and strategy on covert activity in Northern Ireland. Some of this may be excused by the 'in the public interest' mantra, or conveniently and ironically, 'on the grounds of security', but by no means all of it. There were other, more sinister agenda at play: government apologies have started to seep out. Forty years of graphic news bulletins and newspaper headlines told us all about the atrocities perpetrated by the IRA—quite right too—but comparatively less coverage was given to the inequalities meted out to Catholics and nationalists by the British government in the 1960s which were one of the root causes of The Troubles. At the same time, there was comparatively less coverage devoted to the equally savage atrocities perpetrated by the six or so loyalist paramilitary organizations.

In a book like this, with page after page of relentless murders, bombings, lies, hatred, official dissimulation, fake news, partisan claims and bigoted counterclaims, it is easy to lapse into complacency and to become inured to the death and horror that blighted the people of Northern Ireland for so long from 1969. It is important to resist this, if only for the sake of the 3,532 victims, especially the many completely innocent victims whose only mistake was to be in the wrong place at the wrong time and who paid for this supreme misfortune with their lives, or were casually singled out at random and butchered on the assumption that they were on the wrong side of the religious divide from their murderers.

Furthermore, we know—from figures compiled by the Victims Commission—that for every murder there were scores of 'collateral' injured—'survivors' scarred physically and psychologically by bullets, shrapnel and bomb blasts. Their suffering lasts a life time and did not end with the Good Friday Agreement; they are still living with their shattering injuries, their lost limbs and terrified memories that return to haunt them.

Furthermore, we know—again, from the Victims Commission—that for every murder there are dozens of associated casualties: widows and widowers, fiancés and fiancées, brothers, sisters, mothers and fathers, daughters, sons and friends. Many of these will still be living with their eternal grief; many will have had their lives utterly changed by the constant need to look after and care for an injured family member—another life sentence inflicted by the momentary triggering of gun or the unannounced detonation of a nail bomb. All in all, the Victims Commission estimates that something in the region of 500,000 people were affected by The Troubles in Northern Ireland alone.

In declassified papers (file 2017/10/34) first published on Friday, December 29, 2017 we learned that loyalist paramilitaries were encouraged to assassinate Charles Haughey; the Irish prime minister was informed of this in a letter sent to his Dublin office in 1987 by the proscribed Ulster Volunteer Force on headed and official UVF

Children were by no means immune from 'The Troubles'.

notepaper. MI5 actually took the trouble to provide the UVF with 'targeting details'. Haughey was serving his third period as taoiseach. With memories of high-profile political assassinations aboard boats still fresh, the threat was taken seriously by the Irish government: divers were deployed to ensure that the hull of Haughey's yacht was clear of explosives. To the UVF this was nothing new: they claimed to have been regularly exploited and manipulated by MI5, MI6 and British Special Forces between 1972 and 1978 and in 1985. Indeed, the UVF claimed to have killed seventeen men based on information furnished by British intelligence during earlier years of The Troubles. The letter went straight to the point: "In 1985 we were approached by a MI5 officer attached to the NIO [Northern Ireland office] and based in Lisburn. He asked us to execute you." The MI5 operative, a certain Alex Jones, is alleged to have provided details of Haughey's cars, photographs of his home, his private island, Inishvickillane, bought in 1974 which lies off the coast of County Kerry, and of his yacht, *Celtic Mist*. Details of Haughey's trips to Farranfore airport in Kerry and photographs of a plane he used were also given.

The UVF response was unequivocal: "We refused to do it. We were asked would we accept responsibility if you were killed. We refused. We have no love for you but we are not going to carry out work for the Dirty Tricks Department of the British."

As leader of Fianna Fáil, the official opposition party in 1985, Haughey was seen by London as a problem, due to his tough line on nationalist and republican issues. In November 1985 the Anglo-Irish Agreement was signed between Garret FitzGerald and Margaret Thatcher, a concord which gave the Republic of Ireland a formal say in Northern Ireland and its affairs. As with the earlier New Ireland Forum Report, Haughey savagely criticized the Anglo-Irish Agreement pledging to renegotiate it, if re-elected. When that letter, part of a British smear campaign against him focusing on Haughey's supposed extravagant lifestyle, was delivered in Dublin in August 1987, Haughey was on holiday, but on his return he asked for the Irish justice department to look into the letter's claims. It certainly appeared genuine, signed in block capitals 'Capt W. Johnston', the official name used by the UVF in its formal statements. The late Taoiseach's son, Seán Haughey, has told Irish broadcaster, RTÉ, that his family were aware of the death threat and took it seriously.

The objective of the MI5 plot was to destabilize the Republic and destroy the Eire economy. The UVF claimed that British intelligence planned to provide it with a spoonful of each of "Anthras" (sic), "Foort (sic) and Mouth Disease", "Fowl Pest, Swine Fever and Jaagsikpi (sic)", all to be released into Ireland. (Presumably, by 'Jaagsikpi' MI5 was referring to ovine pulmonary adenocarcinoma (OPA), or jaagsiekte, a contagious disease of the lungs found in sheep and goats. OPA is caused by a retrovirus called jaagsiekte sheep retrovirus (JSRV).)

This particular release of declassified papers is important for a number of reasons, not least for the essential information it gives and the light it allegedly shines on the activities of MI5 and the UVF. It also adumbrates the British government's robust attitude and response to a difficult Irish opposition party and its leader, and it confirms for us the ongoing collusion between the British government and loyalist factions in Northern Ireland. Furthermore, it evidences covert British intelligence activity in the Republic and a willingness to shoot to kill on either side of the border, with intended victims extending high up the political ladder. At the same time, it raises the thorny question why British security forces felt the need to implicate the UVF when it had its own resources that were quite capable of carrying out the Haughey assassination.

As such, the declassified release neatly encapsulates the aim and scope of this book: to illuminate issues surrounding shoot-to-kill, murder squads, political assassinations and British government collusion with loyalists. Furthermore, it exposes questions surrounding the veracity of such information: no doubt the letter was written, sent and received, but can we ever be sure that its claims were not a fiction to unnerve a recalcitrant and unenthusiastic Dublin government? Was it perhaps, as some would prefer, just another example of the post-colonial British strutting on the world stage in the deluded belief that they could still tell anyone anywhere to do anything and fully expect it to be done?

The common assumption even today is that in 1969, the so-called Troubles (Na Trioblóidí) in Northern Ireland were simply a straight, clean-cut religious conflict between majority Protestant loyalists and minority Roman Catholic nationalists. In reality, nothing could be further from the truth: events in 1969 and the years before that were just the start of an incipient, complex 'irregular war', a guerrilla war or, bizarrely, a 'low-level' war, a 'low-intensity conflict' with politics, religion, ideology, nationalism and unionism all conspiring to exacerbate and prolong a bloody and unforgiving conflict which occasionally spilled out of Northern Ireland into the Irish Republic and the mainlands of Britain and continental Europe. Some analysts maintain that The Troubles were all about the constitutional status of Northern Ireland and were not a religious conflict at all.

A series of historical events reaching back to 1609, in which the British often acted at best with colonial arrogance and, at worst, with atrocious, oppressive brutality, have never been forgotten, particularly by nationalist Irish men and women. These corrosive events have stoked the fires of simmering discontent for centuries. The number of incompatible and internecine agencies involved, the at times insensitivity and ineptitude of the British government, the often uncooperative, disinterested stance of the Dublin government and the savagery of the protagonists only served to make things much, much worse.

We can be forgiven for this oversimplification, this basic misconception because what the world watched on its televisions every evening and read in its newspapers every morning persuasively and eloquently conveyed a gross over-simplification of the real situation. Obviously, on the one hand the nationalist desire for one Ireland controlled by the minority Catholics and, on the other, the loyalists intent to resist this and remain loyal to the union were elemental. It may surprise some to know, for example, there were two IRAs which clashed in a power struggle and, thereby, further complicated an already intractable situation. This was at the heart of what was really happening in 1969: an intensifying power struggle between rival IRA and Sinn Féin factions and a nationalist desire to end blatant discrimination and social injustices against the Catholic-nationalist minority by the Protestant-unionist government and police force. Simply put, about two-thirds of the traditional IRA, the official Cathal Goulding Group, were persuaded to or felt inclined to move over to the more hard line, more active nationalist Provisional IRA, a force that had its attractions both for older, veteran nationalists and for the militant younger members. Many of these were radical-ized by the 1969 violence and were known as 'sixty-niners'. Various events have been offered as the trigger for the most recent Troubles: the formation of the modern Ulster Volunteer Force (UVF) in 1966, the civil rights march in Derry on October 5, 1968, the 'Battle of the Bogside' on August 12/13, 1969, the politicization of the civil rights movement in Northern Ireland, and the deployment of British troops on August 14, 1969.

To focus their grievances, the Northern Ireland Civil Rights Association (NICRA) was set up in January 1967. June 20, 1968 was a significant day: civil rights activists took their protest against housing discrimination to the next level by setting up a squat in a house in Caledon. The local council had allocated the house to an unmar-ried nineteen-year-old Protestant by the name of Emily Beattie, the secretary of a local UUP politician, instead of to either of two other claimants, both large Catholic families with children. RUC officers—Beattie's brother was one of them—forcibly evicted the activists. Two days before the protest, the two Catholic families who had been squatting in the house next door were removed by police. Austin Currie, a nationalist MP and one of the activists, brought their case to the local council and to Stormont, but had been shown the door. The incident served to energize the civil rights movement.

NICRA held their first march on August 24, 1968, from Coalisland to Dungannon, the first of many. These were immediately characterized first by loyalist attacks on the marchers and counter-demonstrations designed to get the marches banned and, second, a clearly tepid reaction from the police. Nationalists naturally saw the

RUC as supporting the loyalists and turning a collective blind eye to the attacks. On October 5, 1968 things deteriorated when a civil rights march in Derry was banned by the Northern Ireland government; the nationalists defied the ban, RUC officers surrounded the marchers and beat them mercilessly and without provocation leaving more than a hundred people injured, including nationalist politicians. The shameful incident caused outrage among nationalists, and two more days of rioting in Derry. It was filmed and shown on TVs around the world.

On new year's day 1969, People's Democracy—a newly formed student civil rights group—set off on a four-day march from Belfast to Derry, which was incessantly attacked by loyalists. Burntollet Bridge was the site of a concerted assault on the marchers by about 200 or so loyalists, including some off-duty RUC officers, armed with iron bars, bricks and bottles. When the march reached Derry City it was again attacked. The marchers claimed that the police failed to protect them and that some even helped the attackers. That night RUC officers went on a rampage

Free Derry corner, part of the autonomous nationalist area of Free Derry between 1969 and 1972, now demolished. Free Derry Corner was at the corner of Lecky Road and Fahan Street in the Bogside. The slogan was first painted in January 1969 after an unauthorized midnight incursion by RUC men into the Bogside.

in the Bogside area of Derry, attacking Catholic homes, violating and intimidating residents, and hurling sectarian abuse. Residents sealed off the Bogside with barricades to keep the police out, creating 'Free Derry', a no-go area for the security forces.

The British authorities clumsily attempted to suppress the nationalist unrest, only to be accused of the police brutality they brought to the situation, a situation that intensified with loyalist violence, culminating in the August 1969 riots and the deployment of British troops. These troops were initially welcomed by the Catholic community but the goodwill soon evaporated and the army was seen by many Catholics as a hostile, repressive force. This all paved the way for the rise and rise of armed paramilitary organizations on both sides of the political and religious chasm.

Between 1970 and 1972 political violence escalated, reaching a high in 1972 when nearly 500 people, half of them civilians, lost their lives. By the end of 1971, Free Derry was a no-go area with twenty-nine barricades in place; sixteen of these were impenetrable even to the British Army's one-ton armoured vehicles. Many of the nationalist 'no-go areas' were controlled by one of the two factions of the Irish Republican Army: the Provisional IRA and the Official IRA.

Ask a unionist, a loyalist, and he or she will tell you that the prime reason for the explosion in violence was the schism within the IRA leading to the formation of the Provisional Irish Republican Army and the Official Irish Republican Army. The older (Official) IRA was more inclined toward non-violent civil agitation, while the new Provisional IRA was intent on a relentless "armed struggle" against British rule in Northern Ireland as "defenders of the Catholic community". This partisan, sectarian stance embodied a policy of armed conflict against British forces and with anyone who supported British rule, a policy where the deployment of murder squads was axiomatic.

On the other hand, asking nationalists would elicit a response which revealed a number of events which they maintained contributed to the upsurge in violence. The ongoing discrimination against Catholics, sanctioned it would appear by the British, and the blatant partiality of the RUC are obvious; two others are the Falls curfew in July 1970, and the introduction of internment on August 9, 1971. The former involved a situation in which 3,000 troops inflicted a curfew on the nationalist Lower Falls area of Belfast, firing off more than 1,500 rounds of ammunition in gun battles with the Official IRA in which four people died.

The introduction of internment was never going to provide a solution to an increasingly intractable and toxic set of problems. Indeed, internment had quite the opposite effect: it was inflammatory, consigning the North to a vortex of

Mural on Divis Street in remembrance of the Falls Curfew, Belfast, May 2011. (Photo by Ardfern)

all-consuming violence, distrust, destruction and death. The death toll immediately before and following its introduction speaks eloquently: ten people (four British soldiers, four civilians and two republican volunteers) died in the four months leading up to internment; 128 died in the four months after—sixty-nine civilians and fifty-nine 'combatants': thirteen republicans and forty-six British Army, RUC, UDR and loyalist personnel.

The Tally

According to Malcolm Sutton's *Index of Deaths from the Conflict in Ireland*, the definitive work on the subject (CAIN). The Troubles claimed the lives of 3,532 people from 1969 to 2001. Approximately 60% of the dead were killed by republicans, 30% by loyalists and 10% by British security forces. Republican paramilitary groups killed 2,058 people, loyalist paramilitary groups 1,027, British security forces 363, persons unknown seventy-nine and Irish security forces five, with 3,532 the overall tally.

According to another invaluable resource, David McKittrick's *Lost Lives: The stories of the men, women and children who died as a result of the Northern Ireland troubles* (2006), 3,720 people were killed from 1966 to 2006. If that were not bad enough,

The long-term effect of such displays of aggression on some children are surely incalculable.

A Belfast girl holds up a sign NO ENTRY. The caption of this press photo read, "The tragic routine of Belfast: Belfast 1972 ... where barricades—and bomb blasts—are almost commonplace. The young children play a game of their own: the threat of real violence is never far away. Will their generation grow up into a Belfast of peace— or continuing bloodshed?" (Source Camera Press)

Who knows that they're thinking?

257 of the victims were children under the age of seventeen, a shocking 7.2% of the total during this period. The murder squads did not discriminate by age: children were, it seems, fair game.

In *The Politics of Antagonism: Understanding Northern Ireland*, Brendan O'Leary tells us that "nearly two percent of the population of Northern Ireland have been killed or injured through political violence ... If the equivalent ratio of victims to population had been produced in Great Britain in the same period some 100,000 people would have died, and if a similar level of political violence had taken place, the number of fatalities in the USA would have been over 500,000".

Injury figures are just as alarming. In 2010 it was estimated that 107,000 people in Northern Ireland suffered some physical injury as a direct result of the conflict. Using data from the Northern Ireland Statistics and Research Agency, the Victims Commission estimated that the conflict resulted in 500,000 'victims' in Northern Ireland alone. 'Victims' are those who are directly affected by bereavement, physical injury or trauma as a result of the conflict.

There were 363 people killed by British troops in the conflict.

According to Malcolm Sutton's *Index* approximately 52% of the dead were civilians, 32% members/former members of the British security forces, 11% members of republican paramilitaries and 5% members of loyalist paramilitaries. About 60% of the civilian casualties were Catholics, 30% Protestants and the rest were from outside Northern Ireland.

One reviewer said of Sutton's *Index*: "[it] proves that, militarily, the IRA out-fought British armed forces by 1,091 kills to 169; while, as to terrorism, British armed forces murdered 907 non-combatants compared to the IRA/IPLO/INLA's 151 ... It reveals that British spooks and armed forces perpetrated the 1st, 3rd, 4th and 5th deadliest terrorist bombings and shootings; all of which our news media blamed on the IRA."

Of the civilian casualties, 48% were killed by loyalists, 39% were killed by republicans, and 10% were killed by the British security forces. Of those killed by British security forces, 187 (51.5%) were civilians, 145 (39.9%) were republican paramilitaries, 18 (4.9%) were members of loyalist paramilitaries and 13 (3.5%) were fellow members of the British security forces. Of those killed by republican paramilitaries,

Soldiers on patrol in County Armagh in 1998.

1,080 (52%) were members/former members of the British security forces, 723 (35%) were civilians, 187 (9%) were members of republican paramilitaries, 57 (2.7%) were members of loyalist paramilitaries and 11 (0.5%) were members of the Irish security forces. Of those killed by loyalist paramilitaries, 878 (85.4%) were civilians, 94 (9%) were members of loyalist paramilitaries, 41 (4%) were members of republican para-militaries and 14 (1%) were members of the British security forces.

While republican paramilitaries were responsible for the greatest number of deaths in total, they caused fewer civilian deaths than loyalist paramilitaries, and had a lower civilian-to-combatant casualty ratio than either of the other two belligerents.

Several casualties listed as civilians were later claimed by the IRA as their members. One Ulster Defence Association (UDA) and three Ulster Volunteer Force (UVF) members killed during the conflict were also Ulster Defence Regiment (UDR) soldiers at the time of their deaths. At least one civilian victim was an off-duty member of the Territorial Army: Robert Dunseath, killed in the Teebane massacre was a member of the Royal Irish Rangers (Royal Irish Rangers roll of honour, royalirishrangers.co.uk. Retrieved January 31, 2018).

According to Malcolm Sutton's *Index of Deaths from the Conflict in Ireland: Status of Person Killed.* (CAIN): civilians (including civilian political activists) 1,841, British security force personnel (serving and former members) 1,114, British Army (including UDR, RIR and TA) 757, RUC 319, Northern Ireland Prison Service 26, English police forces 6, Royal Air Force 4, Royal Navy 2, Irish security force personnel 11, Garda Síochána 9, Irish army 1, Irish Prison Service 1, members of republican paramilitaries 396, members of loyalist paramilitaries 170.

According to Malcolm Sutton's *Index of Deaths from the Conflict in Ireland: Geographical Location of the Death.* (CAIN): Belfast 1,541, West Belfast 623, North Belfast 577, South Belfast 213, East Belfast 128, County Armagh 477, County Tyrone 340, County Down 243, Derry City 227, County Antrim 209, County Londonderry 123 County Fermanagh 112, Republic of Ireland 116, England 125 and Continental Europe 18.

Who died when: 16 in 1969, 26 in 1970, 171 in 1971, 480 in 1972 (the highest toll), 255 in 1973, 294 in 1974, 260 in 1975, 297 in 1976, 110 in 1977, 82 in 1978, 121 in 1979, 80 in 1980, 114 in 1981, 111 in 1982, 84 in 1983, 69 in 1984, 57 in 1985, 61 in 1986, 98 in 1987, 104 in 1988, 76 in 1989, 81 in 1990, 97 in 1991, 88 in 1992, 88 in 1993, 64 in 1994, 9 in 1995, 18 in 1996, 22 in 1997, 55 in 1998, 8 in 1999, 19 in 2000, 16 in 2001 and 20 in 2002.

The activities of both nationalist and loyalist paramilitary organizations clearly show that the death or murder squad was an essential and enduring weapon in their various campaigns. The death squad and its associations with shoot-to-kill policies within the British security agencies is much more contentious and controversial.

One of the 16,209 bombings during The Troubles.

Nevertheless, the evidence shows that, at least in certain individual operations like Operation Flavius in Gibraltar and at Loughgall, SAS murder squads were dispatched with orders to eliminate their targets: there was very little prospect of arrests being made or prisoners taken. Proven collusion between the British security forces and loyalist insurgents only served to muddy further already murky waters by implicating the British in the murder of (mainly) nationalists by loyalist death squads—in short, murder by proxy and by association.

PART 1: NATIONALIST PARAMILITARY ORGANIZATIONS

Nationalist paramilitary organizations years active / operational

Continuity Irish Republican Army (CIRA)	1994 to present
Irish National Liberation Army (INLA)	1974–2009
Irish People's Liberation Organization (IPLO)	1986–1992
Official Irish Republican Army (OIRA)	1970–1972
Óglaigh na hÉireann (ONH) (Real IRA splinter group)	2009 to present
Provisional Irish Republican Army (PIRA)	1970–2005
Real Irish Republican Army (RIRA)	1997 to present
Saor Éire (SÉ)	1967–1975

Provisional Irish Republican Army

"We declare our allegiance to the 32 county Irish republic, proclaimed at Easter 1916, established by the first Dáil Éireann in 1919, overthrown by forces of arms in 1922 and suppressed to this day by the existing British-imposed six-county and twenty-six-county partition states."

IRA mission statement, December 28, 1969

In many ways the Provisional IRA (Óglaigh na hÉireann) defined The Troubles; they were never far away from many of the nationalist murders, bombings and shootings in Northern Ireland and on the mainlands of the UK and Europe. The carnage and misery the IRA wreaked—human and economic—is incalculable. Given their mandate, to force the United Kingdom to negotiate a withdrawal from Northern Ireland and to destroy anyone that got in their way, this is hardly surprising. So, they shot and bombed their way through The Troubles, ever true to their cause, constantly energized by frantic paper-selling and viewer-fixated British media coverage—the 'oxygen of publicity'—while at the same time

The funeral of Seán South, 5 January 1957. South (1928–57) was a member of an IRA unit led by Sean Garland on a raid against a Royal Ulster Constabulary barracks in Brookeborough, County Fermanagh on New Year's Day, 1957. He died of wounds sustained during the raid along with another IRA volunteer, Fergal O'Hanlon.

enraged by that same media's plainly imbalanced coverage that assigned to them the lion's share of the atrocities when the loyalists were equally culpable in many respects.

Cathal Goulding (1923–1998) was Official IRA chief of staff from 1962 to 1972. He was responsible for repositioning the IRA further to the left in the 1960s, opposed the policy of abstentionism and inculcated a Marxist interpretation of Irish politics. The focus was on class struggle and its aim was to unite the Irish nationalist and unionist working classes in order to overthrow capitalism, both British and Irish. The Official IRA, like the Provisional IRA, conducted an armed campaign but Goulding argued that this ultimately divided the Irish working class. After public outrage and horror at the shooting of William Best and the bombing of the Aldershot barracks, the Official IRA announced a ceasefire in 1972.

Ranger William Best died in the wake of Bloody Sunday in 1972 in which the British Army shot dead fourteen unarmed civilians. Best (19) was a local Derry man home on leave from the British Army in Germany, staying at his parents' house in the Creggan. He was abducted, interrogated and summarily shot by the Official IRA. The following day, 500 women marched on the Republican Club offices in protest. Nine days later, on May 29, the Official IRA declared their ceasefire. The Provisional IRA initially declined to follow suit, but after informal approaches to the British government they announced a ceasefire from June 26.

When British troops disembarked in Belfast in 1969 they were welcomed by Protestants and Catholics alike: the army signified protection against sectarian

This photo was taken by the Irish photographer Colman Doyle. The original caption: "A woman IRA volunteer on active service in West Belfast with an AR-18 assault rifle."

attacks; the nationalists had no trust in the RUC. Soldiers were plied with tea and toast in the Catholic Falls Road area of west Belfast; these encouraging images were shown all around the world and gave signs of hope.

Seemingly the British government was at pains to do "nothing that would suggest partiality to one section of the community"; relations between the army and the local population were at a high following army assistance with flood relief in August 1970. However, the Falls curfew and a situation that was insensitively described at the time as "an inflamed sectarian one, which is being deliberately exploited by the IRA and other extremists" ensured that the hospitality did not last for very long. Protestants soon saw the army as their exclusive protectors against the Provisional IRA while to many Catholics the army was an oppressive force supporting unionist rule. One senior NCO tells, in John Lindsay's *Brits Speak Out: British Soldiers' Impressions of the Northern Ireland Conflict* how "On the other [republican] side, some of the people whose homes we'd have to search would be as nice as pie. Once the curtains were drawn they would chat to you and make you cups of tea."

Nothing exceptional about that you might say, but in Ireland, north and south, a cup of tea is a potent symbol of friendship and hospitality. Less attractively, Royal Military Police investigations into over 150 killings by the army in the early 1970s were known as "tea and sandwich inquiries" to denote the casual, shabby nature of the inquiries and the cozy relationship that existed between the RUC and the army.

The Troubles were never the 'people's war' they are often described as: the Protestant majority (65% at the time) was fervently against nationalist terrorism; many in the Catholic minority, while ideologically supportive, were against violent means.

A key policy of the Provisional IRA and of Sinn Féin was to foster urban insurgency, civil disorder which would seriously exercise and strain routine policing and thus create a threat to national security and advance their desire for a one-Ireland island. Sinn Féin worked quietly in the background to manipulate civil rights groups towards a more nationalist agenda while their brothers in the Provisionals provoked sectarian tension with gusto. Catholics fighting Protestants in the streets of the North was good PR for the Provos and a highly effective recruiting sergeant. Police confrontation with civil rights protesters was then sold by Sinn Féin as attacks on nationalists by a police force that was anti-Catholic, thus destroying any pre-existing cross-community element in the civil rights movement and driving a wedge between Catholics and Protestants.

The Civil Rights movement

The non-violent civil rights campaign has its roots in the mid-1960s, a collection of groups like the Northern Ireland Civil Rights Association (NICRA), the Campaign for Social Justice (CSJ), the Derry Citizens' Action Committee (DCAC) and People's Democracy. Their collective objectives were an end to job discrimination—there was evidence that Catholics/nationalists were less likely to get certain jobs, especially jobs in local government; an end to discrimination in housing allocation—there was evidence that unionist-controlled local councils allocated housing to Protestants before Catholics/nationalists; introduction of universal one man, one vote—in Northern Ireland, only householders could vote in local elections, while in the rest of the United Kingdom all adults had the franchise. The discrimination in housing provision disenfranchised more Catholics than Protestants; an end to gerrymandering of electoral boundaries which meant that nationalists had less voting power than unionists, even where nationalists were a majority; reform of the Royal Ulster Constabulary which was over 90% Protestant and notorious for sectarianism and police brutality; repeal of the Special Powers Act—this allowed police to search without a warrant, arrest and imprison people without charge or trial, ban any assemblies or parades, and ban any publications; the Act was being used almost exclusively against nationalists.

Another aspect typical of the disrupting insurgency was the IRA's policy of bombing local businesses to deter inward investment and job creation in the province. Inevitably, the stones and petrol bombs were exchanged for bombs and bullets, and for premeditated sectarian murder and torture. The killing squads had arrived.

In its pursuit of Irish republicanism down the years, the IRA has taken on many forms. It first emerged in the Fenian raids on British towns and forts in the late 1700s and 1860s. Between 1917 and 1922 the Irish Republican Army (the 'Old' IRA) was recognized as the legitimate army of the Irish Republic; in April 1921 the first split followed the signing of the Anglo-Irish Treaty, with supporters of the treaty forming the nucleus of the National Army of the newly created Irish Free State (also known as the government forces or the regulars and later known as the Irish Defence Forces), while the anti-treaty forces continued to use the name Irish Republican Army, (the Republicans, Irregulars or Executive forces).

The anti-treaty wing of the Irish Republican Army (1922–69) fought and lost the civil war (1922–23) and consequently refused to recognize either the Irish Free State or Northern Ireland, preferring to see them as creations of British imperialism. It existed in one form or another for over forty years before the split in 1969.

In the 1930s, the remainder of the IRA, including that part of the Old IRA organized within Northern Ireland, started a bombing campaign in Britain, a campaign in Northern Ireland and some military activities in the Free State (later the Republic of Ireland). The relationship between Sinn Féin and the IRA was re-established in the late 1930s

The original Official IRA (OIRA), what was left of the IRA after the 1969 schism, was largely marxist and became inactive militarily while its political wing, Official Sinn Féin, became the Workers' Party of Ireland. The Provisional IRA (PIRA) seceded from the OIRA in 1969 over abstentionism and how to deal with the increasingly violent Troubles. Despite being unsympathetic to OIRA's marxism, it developed a left-wing orientation and increasing political activity. The Continuity IRA (CIRA), broke from PIRA in 1986 because the latter ended its policy on abstentionism, thus recognizing the authority of the Republic of Ireland. The Real IRA (RIRA) was a 1997 breakaway from PIRA consisting of members opposed to the Northern Ireland peace process.

In April 2011, former members of the Provisional IRA announced a resumption of hostilities, and that they "had now taken on the mantle of the mainstream IRA". They also claimed, "We continue to do so under the name of the Irish Republican Army. We are the IRA" and insisted that they "were entirely separate from the Real IRA, Óglaigh na hÉireann [ONH] and the Continuity IRA". They claimed responsibility for the April killing of PSNI constable Ronan Kerr as well as responsibility for other attacks that had previously been claimed by the Real IRA and ONH. There has been sporadic violence since the Good Friday Agreement of April 1998, including a campaign by anti-ceasefire republicans.

The Troubles turned out to be the longest significant campaign in the history of the British Army. The British government has always maintained that its forces were neutral in the conflict, fighting to uphold law and order in Northern Ireland and the right of the people of Northern Ireland to democratic self-determination. Nationalists saw it differently, viewing the state forces as forces of occupation or partisan combatants. Key findings by the Police Ombudsman's Operation Ballast investigation—a three-and-a-half-year investigation into a series of complaints about police conduct in relation to the murder of Raymond McCord Junior in November 1997—confirmed that the RUC and Special Branch colluded more than once with loyalist paramilitaries, were involved in murder and obstructed the course of justice when claims of collusion and murder were investigated

So, we have a conflict which, right from the start, makes routine use of murder squads which are characterized at times by a shoot-to-kill mandate championed by various paramilitary organizations, the police and the British Army.

The violence exploded between the years 1970 to 1972, peaking in 1972 when nearly 500 people, just over half of them civilians, died in those three years. By the end of 1971 there were twenty-nine barricades in place in Derry, blocking access to Free Derry. The IRA planted nearly 1,800 bombs—an average of five a day—in 1972. In 1972 there were more than 10,600 shootings in Northern Ireland.

Unionists, of course, blamed the violence squarely on the Provisional IRA and the now separate Official IRA. The older IRA had espoused non-violent civil unrest but the Provisional IRA was intent on waging 'armed struggle' against British rule to gain their ends. The new Provisional IRA took on the role of 'defenders of the Catholic community', splitting the community rather than doing anything to bring it together. The 1971 introduction of internment without trial didn't help; of the

One of many IRA funerals in the 1970s.

British troops on the Shankill Road in 1970.

first 350 detainees, none was Protestant. To add insult to injury, sloppy intelligence and operational bungling ensured that precious few of those interned were actually republican activists at the time of their arrest.

The RUC was the first security force to suffer at the hands of the Provisional IRA when in August 1970 two constables were murdered in a bomb attack in South Armagh; six months later the army had its first casualty: Lance-Corporal Robert Curtis was killed by a sniper's bullet in Belfast.

By 1971, however, the Official IRA was largely sidelined; they had agreed with the Provisionals on the legitimization of murdering RUC Special Branch officers but not regular RUC officers. Official policy directed that the Provisional IRA/Sinn Féin tolerated no RUC and no collaborators ('touts') or anyone they considered to be a collaborator. Altogether there were eighty-three extrajudicial executions—seventy-eight Catholics and five Protestants—from January 1971. The youngest victim was fifteen—his body was displayed in the street as a horrific deterrent; the oldest a pensioner of sixty-eight who took multiple gunshots to the head in his back garden. Husband and wife Gerard and Catherine Mahon were shot together.

The IRA has the unenviable record of executing every member of the security forces they held prisoner, 'out-slaying' even so-called Islamic State. Of the eighty-three so-called collaborators executed, fifty-three (70%) were civilians, twenty-six were terrorists; all were Catholics. Four of the male civilians had learning disabilities and three of the civilians were women. Executions peaked in 1973. Attending a wounded soldier or policeman qualified as collaboration, as Jean McConville (37) discovered in December 1972: a Catholic widowed mother of ten, her body was not discovered until 2003, in the Republic. The sad, sorry complete list, with disturbing details including torture and booby-trapping bodies, can be found in William Matchett's *Secret Victory*, pp. 47-59.

Loyalists, of course, were not in any way innocent. They murdered nineteen or more people, all Protestants, suspected of collaboration, half of them civilians, half loyalist terrorists.

The 'Long War'

The 1977 edition of the *Green Book*, an IRA induction and training manual, describes the murderous intent in the strategy of the 'Long War', a campaign initiated after the failure of the 1975 ceasefire: A war of attrition against enemy personnel [British Army] based on causing as many deaths as possible so as to create a demand from their [the British] people at home for their withdrawal; a bombing campaign aimed at making the enemy's financial interests in our country unprofitable while at the same time curbing long-term investment in our country; to make the Six Counties ... ungovernable except by colonial military rule; to sustain the war and gain support for its ends by National and International propaganda and publicity campaigns and; by defending the war of liberation by punishing criminals, collaborators and informers.

The 1970s ended in terrible carnage, perpetrated by the Provisional IRA. In February 1979 a former prison officer and his wife were murdered by the Provisional IRA in Belfast. On March 22 the IRA killed the British ambassador to the Netherlands, Richard Sykes, and his Dutch valet in a gun attack in Den Haag in the Netherlands. On the same day the IRA carried out twenty-four bombings across Northern Ireland.

On August 27, 1979, Lord Louis Mountbatten (79) was holidaying in Mullaghmore, County Sligo, when he was killed by a bomb planted on board his boat. Three other people died in the explosion: Baroness Doreen Bradbourne (83), the elderly mother of Mountbatten's son-in-law; Nicholas Knatchbull (14), a grandson of Mountbatten, and a local boy, Paul Maxwell (15). The same day, eighteen British soldiers, mostly members of the Parachute Regiment, were killed by two remote-controlled bombs in a deadly cross-border ambush at Warrenpoint, County Down.

The hunger strikes of 1981 gifted the IRA seven martyrs who were to become rebel celebrities. It also demonstrated the extent of the IRA's popularity when no fewer than 100,000 people attended Bobby Sands's funeral mass in West Belfast while thousands mourned at the funerals of the other hunger-strikers. Three members of the INLA also died in the hunger strikes.

The IRA's capability to continue its campaign of murder was boosted with arms donations smuggled into the Republic by Libya's Muammar Gaddafi, enraged no doubt at the Thatcher government for facilitating the Reagan administration's bombing of Tripoli, an action which killed one of Gaddafi's children. Money from pro-IRA partisans in the United States and elsewhere continued to pour in. Death was certainly the intention on October 12, 1984 when the IRA detonated a 100-pound bomb in the

The funeral of Bobby Sands, May 7, 1981.

The Bobby Sands mural on the gable wall of the Sinn Féin offices on the Falls Road, Belfast.

Ardoyne, Belfast: hunger strike mural.

Grand Hotel in Brighton where politicians including Prime Minister Thatcher were staying for the Conservative Party conference. The bomb killed five people, including Conservative MP Sir Anthony Berry and the wife of government chief whip John Wakeham; thirty-four others were injured.

The Grand Hotel in Brighton following the IRA bomb attack. The photo was taken on the morning of October 12, 1984, some hours after the blast.

A particularly shameful day was November 8, 1987 when a Provisional IRA time bomb exploded during a Remembrance Day parade to commemorate victims of the Great War, in Enniskillen, County Fermanagh. The bomb exploded by a cenotaph killing eleven people—ten civilians, including a pregnant woman, and one serving member of the RUC—and injuring sixty-three. Former school headmaster Ronnie Hill was seriously injured in the bombing and existed in a coma for more than a decade before his death in December 2000. The IRA eventually apologized for the atrocity, claiming that it had been a mistake and that its target had been the British soldiers on parade. The unit responsible was disbanded. Loyalist paramilitaries retaliated with revenge attacks on Catholics, mostly civilians. Another IRA bomb had been planted at nearby Tullyhommon at the Remembrance Day commemoration there but it failed to go off.

Four months later, three unarmed IRA volunteers were shot dead by SAS soldiers at a Shell petrol station on Winston Churchill Avenue in Gibraltar during Operation Flavius. Their funeral was held at Belfast's Milltown cemetery and was attacked by Michael Stone, a lone-wolf member of the UDA who threw grenades and fired shots as the coffins were lowered. The attack killed three people, including an IRA volunteer. Stone was jailed for life but freed eleven years later under the Good Friday Agreement.

The consequences of Gibraltar continued to resonate when on March 19, 1988 two British soldiers in civilian clothes, David Howes and Derek Wood, the driver, inadvertently drove into the funeral procession in Andersonstown of Caoimhín Mac Brádaigh, one of the three people murdered three days earlier by loyalist Michael Stone. The cortège was proceeding along the Andersonstown Road towards

Corporal David Howes, one of two British soldiers killed in west Belfast on March 19, 1988.

Milltown cemetery. The corporals, assigned to the Det, were seemingly on a routine patrol. Republicans understandably thought that this was another loyalist attack. Blocked from escape by black taxis, the soldiers were dragged from their armoured car, a silver Volkswagen Passat hatchback, stripped and found to be armed. They were taken away and shot by the Provisional IRA. This became known as the Corporals' Killings.

In 1987, the Irish People's Liberation Organization (IPLO) entered the fray. A breakaway faction of the INLA, it began a bloody and debilitating feud against the INLA. By 1992, the IPLO had been neutralized by the Provisional IRA for its involvement in drug-trafficking.

Since the 1970s the South Armagh Brigade of the IRA had used Crossmaglen and neighbouring villages as their stronghold. In February 1978, a British Army Gazelle helicopter was shot down near Silverbridge, killing Lieutenant-Colonel Ian Corden-Lloyd.

In the 1990s, the IRA formed a new strategy to restrict British Army foot patrols around Crossmaglen. Two sniper teams were deployed to attack British Army and RUC patrols, firing from an improvised armoured car using a .50 BMG-calibre M82 sniper rifle. The snipers killed seven soldiers and two constables. The last man to be killed before the Good Friday Agreement was a British soldier, Bombardier Steven Restorick.

1990 saw another Gazelle flying over the border between Tyrone and Monaghan shot down; there were no fatalities.

The Teebane massacre happened on January 17, 1992 between Omagh and Cookstown in County Tyrone when a roadside bomb—an estimated 600 pounds (270kg) of homemade explosives in two plastic barrels—obliterated a Ford Transit van carrying fourteen Protestant construction workers working for Karl Construction, based in Antrim and contracted to make repairs to a British Army base in Omagh. The IRA detonated the bomb from about a hundred yards away using a command wire. Eight of the men were killed and the rest injured. The Provisional Irish Republican Army claimed responsibility, saying that the workers were killed because they were "collaborating" with the "forces of occupation". The Teebane incident was part of the IRA policy of executing those working for the British government in the province. Seamus McAvoy (46) was the first to die as a victim of this policy; he was a Catholic shot dead at his home in Dublin for selling portable buildings to the RUC. In October 1990, the IRA launched three 'proxy bomb' attacks. Three contractors were tied into cars full of explosives and ordered to drive to British Army checkpoints while their families were held at gunpoint. The bombs were then remotely detonated. Six soldiers and one of the drivers were killed in the first two attacks. A third proxy bomb was driven to Lisanelly British Army base in Omagh, but the bomb failed to explode. Between August 1985 and January 1992, the IRA killed at least twenty-three people who had been working for or offering services to the security forces.

In the battle of Newry Road in September 1993 a further two British helicopters were damaged in the running firefight. Two more helicopters, an army Lynx and an RAF Puma, were shot down by improvised mortar fire the following year. 1994 was a tense and bloody year, but it did produce a ceasefire. Before this, however, the UDA and UVF stepped up their attacks. The IRA retaliated with the Shankill Road bombing in October 1993, aimed at assassinating the UDA leadership, but it did far worse when it succeeded in butchering eight Protestant civilian shoppers and one low-ranking UDA member, as well as one of the bombers when the bomb detonated prematurely. The UDA retaliated with mass shootings in nationalist areas such as Greysteel and Castlerock. Twelve people died here, all but two of whom were Catholic.

On June 16, 1994, just before the ceasefires, the Irish National Liberation Army murdered a member of the UVF in a shooting on the Shankill Road. In revenge, three days later, the UVF killed six civilians in a shooting at a pub in Loughinisland, County Down. The IRA slew four senior loyalist paramilitaries, three from the UDA and one from the UVF. On August 31, 1994, the IRA declared a ceasefire. The loyalist paramilitaries, temporarily united in the 'Combined Loyalist Military Command', reciprocated six weeks later. Although these ceasefires did not hold, they marked an end to the widespread violence and opened the door to the Good Friday Agreement of 1998.

Eighteen people, all Catholics, including one British Army officer, all males, except for Jean McConville (a convert) and Lisa Dorrian, were kidnapped and killed during The Troubles. They are significant because seventeen of them

The destruction caused by the Omagh bombing, a car bombing that took place on August 15, 1998 in Omagh, County Tyrone. It was carried out by a group calling themselves the Real Irish Republican Army, an IRA splinter group that opposed the IRA's ceasefire and the Good Friday Agreement.

Provisional IRA attacks abroad

1970s: Aldershot bombing (16th Parachute Brigade HQ), Old Bailey bombing, King's Cross and Euston stations, M62 coach bombing, Parliament bombing, Guildford pub bombings, Birmingham bombings, pillar box bombs, Oxford Street bombing, Caterham bombing, London Hilton bombing, Green Park bombing, Balcombe Street siege, British ambassador to the Netherlands and his Dutch valet killed in a gun attack in Den Haag, four British soldiers wounded in bomb detonation under a bandstand in Brussels.

1980s: Hyde Park and Regent's Park bombings, Harrods bombing, barracks bombings at Woolwich, Inglis and Deal, Brighton bombing, British soldier shot dead outside his home, Bielefeld (West Germany), 31 people injured in a car-bomb attack at Rheindahlen military complex, near Mönchengladbach (Germany).

1990s: Lichfield shooting, Downing Street attack, Victoria and Paddington station bombings, London Bridge bombing, Manchester bombing, Warrington bombings, Bishopsgate bombing, Heathrow mortar attacks, Docklands bombing, Manchester bombing, Roermond, (Netherlands) killings, army major shooting Osnabrück barracks (Dortmund, Germany).

(all but Dorrian) were abducted and killed by republicans. Dorrian is thought to have been abducted by loyalists. The Provisional IRA admitted to being involved in the forced disappearance of nine of the sixteen. British Army officer Robert Nairac of the Det, who disappeared from South Armagh, was a Mauritius-born Roman Catholic. As of September 2017, the remains of three of the victims are still missing.

The IRA claimed responsibility for more deaths than any other organization during The Troubles. According to the *Conflict Archive on the Internet* (CAIN), the IRA was responsible for at least 1,707 deaths, about 48% of the total conflict deaths in the conflict. Of these, at least 1,009 (about 59%) were members or former members of the British security forces, and at least 508 (about 29%) were civilians. Over a hundred IRA members were accidentally killed by their own bombs or shot by the IRA for being or suspected of being British agents or informers. Overall, the IRA was responsible for 87–90% of the total British security force deaths, and 27–30% of the total civilian deaths in the conflict.

A powerful show of IRA arms.

Just under 300 IRA members were killed in The Troubles; we can add between fifty and sixty members of Sinn Féin who were also killed. It is estimated that roughly 8,000 people passed through the IRA in the first twenty years of its existence; many who left did so following arrest (senior officers were required to surrender their post after being arrested), retiring from the armed campaign, or "disillusionment".

Irish National Liberation Army

The Irish National Liberation Army (INLA, Arm Saoirse Náisiúnta na hÉireann) was founded in December 1974 by former members of the 'Official' IRA opposed to the Official IRA's 1972 ceasefire. It saw itself as an Irish republican socialist paramilitary group with the stated aim to remove Northern Ireland from the United Kingdom and create a socialist republic encompassing the whole of Ireland. It was the paramilitary wing of the Irish Republican Socialist Party (IRSP). The Official IRA was intent on strangling the INLA at birth.

The INLA first went by the name of the People's Liberation Army or People's Republican Army. Its stated enemies were the British Army and Royal Ulster Constabulary (RUC); it was also active to a small extent in the Republic of Ireland and England. It claimed among its high-profile attacks the Droppin' Well bombing,

INLA volunteers carrying the flag of Ireland, an unidentified red flag and the Starry Plough in the Bogside area of Derry. (Photo by Joel Högberg)

the 1994 Shankill Road killings and the assassinations of Airey Neave in 1979 and Billy Wright in 1997.

The INLA was always a smaller and less active force than the Provisional IRA, constantly weakened by internal feuds. It also appeared to lack unity and cohesion, and inconsistent branding: when the INLA refused to claim responsibility for certain attacks members of the group used the cover names People's Liberation Army (PLA), People's Republican Army (PRA), Armagh People's Republican Army and Catholic Reaction Force (CRF).

After twenty-four years of armed struggle, the INLA announced a ceasefire on August 22, 1998. A year later it stated, "There is no political or moral argument to justify a resumption of the campaign." In October 2009, the INLA vowed to pursue its aims through peaceful political means and decommissioned its weapons. The party now prefers to support a 'No First Strike' policy, namely showing the failure of the peace process without military intervention.

Smaller and less active though it was, the INLA was just as deadly as the IRA when it came to dispensing murder. 1975 started with a flurry of tit-for tat murders: February 20, 1975 saw INLA's Hugh Ferguson, an Irish Republican Socialist Party (IRSP) branch chairperson, the first to be killed in the feud. This was avenged by the INLA with the shooting of OIRA leader Sean Garland in Dublin on March 1. He was shot six times and survived. More shootings brought a truce but it was short-lived: Billy McMillen, the commander of the OIRA in Belfast, was shot by INLA member Gerard Steenson, a murder that was officially unauthorized and condemned by Seamus Costello, the INLA's most competent political and military leader. More assassinations followed on both sides, the most prominent victim being Costello himself, gunned down on the North Strand Road in Dublin on October 6, 1977.

The INLA power base was in and around the Divis Flats in west Belfast; in the late 1970s and early 1980s, the INLA started to compete with the Provisional IRA for members. They first won international notoriety with the assassination on March 30, 1979 of Airey Neave MP, the British Conservative Party's shadow spokesman on Northern Ireland and a close political ally of Margaret Thatcher's. Using inside information, an INLA unit gained access to the House of Commons underground carpark posing as workmen, carrying their device in a toolbox. They affixed a magnetic car bomb with a ball bearing tilt-switch to the floor panel of the driver's seat of Neave's Vauxhall Cavalier which exploded at 2.58 p.m. as Neave drove up the ramp out of the car park: the mercury tilted, completed the circuit and the sixteen ounces of explosive in the bomb detonated. The blast pushed Neave forward, severed his legs and trapped him in the wreckage. Emergency services took almost thirty minutes to free him; he died some eight minutes after his arrival at hospital. Neave's hard-line, belligerent policy which involved greater tactical use of the SAS had made him an obvious target.

This is the INLA statement published in the August 1979 edition of *The Starry Plough*: "In March, retired terrorist and supporter of capital punishment, Airey Neave, got a taste of his own medicine when an INLA unit pulled off the operation of the decade and blew him to bits inside the 'impregnable' Palace of Westminster. The nauseous Margaret Thatcher snivelled on television that he was an 'incalculable loss'—and so he was—to the British ruling class."

The following year, the INLA lost another founding member when Ronnie Bunting, the group's military leader and a Protestant nationalist, was assassinated at his home along with Noel Lyttle, another Protestant member of the INLA; the INLA claimed that the SAS was implicated in the killings. Bunting's father, Ronald Bunting, a dedicated Ulster loyalist, had been a major in the British Army. Despite their differences, father and son remained close. This murder was particularly chilling: at about

4.30 a.m. on October 15, 1980, several balaclava'd UDA gunmen burst into Bunting Junior's house, shot Bunting, his wife Suzanne and Noel Lyttle, a friend. *The Guardian* reported: "The shots woke the Buntings' children, age 7 and 3, who ran screaming into the street after discovering their parents lying together at the top of the stairs, covered in blood. Mr Lyttle was shot in bed, near a cot in which the Buntons' baby son was sleeping." Suzanne Bunting was shot in the face; she survived her horrific injuries.

Soon after, Miriam Daly, another prominent INLA member, was killed by UDA loyalists. *The Irish Times* reported how members of the UDA got into her home intent on killing her husband, James Daly, also a republican activist. Miriam Daly was tied up but James Daly failed to come home as expected as he was in Dublin at the time. After some time, the UDA decided to murder Miriam Daly instead and, muffling the sound of the gun with a cushion, shot her in the head and cut the phone lines before fleeing. Her ten-year-old daughter found the body when she got home from school.

The INLA got their high-profile martyrs when, in the 1980 and 1981 hunger strikes to win the recognition of the political status of paramilitary prisoners, three INLA members died—Patsy O'Hara, Kevin Lynch, and Michael Devine—along with seven members of the Provisional IRA.

In 1982 the INLA bombed the domes at Mount Gabriel radar station in west County Cork, which they wrongly believed was eavesdropping on them to help NATO and thus compromise Irish neutrality.

Their most heinous attack took place on December 6, 1982: the Ballykelly disco bombing of the Droppin' Well Bar in Ballykelly, near Derry, a favourite haunt of British military personnel from Shackleton Barracks, Battalion HQ and HQ Company of the 5th Battalion, Ulster Defence Regiment, close by. Eleven soldiers and six civilians died that night; thirty people were injured. Around 150 people thronged the pub for the regular Monday-night disco. The bomb was estimated at between five and ten pounds of Frangex, small enough to fit into a handbag and left beside a support pillar and, when it exploded at about 23.15 p.m., bringing down the roof, many of the victims were crushed by the falling ceiling. No warning was given. Five of the dead civilians were young women and three—Alan Callaghan, Valerie McIntyre and Angela Maria Hoole—were teenagers. That night Angela Hoole was celebrating her engagement to one of the soldiers who survived the incident. Of the eleven soldiers killed, eight were from the 1st Battalion Cheshire Regiment, two from the Catering Corps and one from the Light Infantry. Four INLA members—Anna Moore, Eamon Moore, Helena Semple and Patrick Shotter—received life sentences for the attack in June 1986. (Anna Moore later married loyalist Bobby Corry while they were in prison.)

The destruction.

November 20, 1983 was the day of the Darkley massacre, a callous gun attack near the village of Darkley in County Armagh, three miles north of the border with the Irish Republic. Three INLA gunmen gunned down worshippers during a church service at Mountain Lodge Pentecostal Church, killing three Protestant civilians and wounding seven. The attackers were disaffected members of the INLA operating under the cover name Catholic Reaction Force, purporting to be operating in retaliation for recent sectarian attacks on Catholics by the loyalist Protestant Action Force (PAF), itself a cover name often used by members of the Ulster Volunteer Force (UVF). The revenge attack was triggered when Catholic civilian Adrian Carroll (24), the brother of an INLA member, Roderick, shot at a roadblock a year earlier, was shot in the head on his doorstep in Armagh on November 8, for which four British soldiers were later convicted of murder. Three church elders were killed as they stood in a doorway handing out Bibles when the murderers approached the building and sprayed it with bullets, wounding a further seven in the sixty-strong congregation before escaping, leaving blood-stained Bibles in their wake, and firing more shots at the horrified worshipers through the wooden walls of the church. As it happened, the service that day was being recorded: the congregation can be heard well into the hymn 'Are You Washed in the Blood of the Lamb?', accompanied by the sound of gunfire. About thirty spent cartridge cases were recovered at the scene.

On December 5 the PAF executed INLA member Joseph Craven (26) in Newtownabbey. The feuding continued. In 1987 the INLA were attacked by the Irish People's Liberation Organization (IPLO), a group formed from expelled or disaffected members of the INLA. This caused the death of sixteen INLA and IPLO members and only ended in 1992 when the Provisional IRA moved in and exterminated the Belfast leadership of the IPLO because of their involvement in drug-dealing. On April 14, 1992, the INLA murdered a sergeant in Derby as he was leaving a British Army recruiting office.

Billy Wright, founder and leader of the Loyalist Volunteer Force (LVF) was assassinated by the INLA in December 1997. Wright was a born-again Christian and former preacher. From July 1996, the LVF had killed fourteen or more Catholic civilians in random gun or bomb attacks. On the morning of December 27, 1997, Wright, then a prisoner in the Maze, was assassinated by three INLA prisoners, Christopher 'Crip' McWilliams, John 'Sonny' Glennon and John Kennaway, armed with two pistols, as he travelled in a prison van with another LVF prisoner, Norman Green, and a prison officer. After killing Wright with seven shots, the three volunteers handed themselves over to prison guards. It has been alleged that Wright, like his predecessor, was an agent of the RUC Special Branch and that his murder was facilitated by collusion with the security forces.

That night, LVF gunmen opened fire on a disco in a mainly nationalist area of Dungannon. Four civilians were wounded and a former Provisional IRA volunteer was killed in the attack.

According to Sutton, the INLA was responsible for at least 120 killings during The Troubles, between 1969 and 2001. This includes those claimed by the so-called People's Liberation Army and People's Republican Army. According to *Lost Lives* (2006), it was responsible for 127 killings. The CAIN database says there were 39 INLA members killed during the conflict, while *Lost Lives* puts the figure at 44 killed. Of those killed by the INLA: 46 (38%) members or former members of the British security forces, including 26 British military personnel and 1 former soldier; 13 Royal Ulster Constabulary officers and 4 former officers; 2 Northern Ireland Prison Service officers; 44 (36%) civilians, including politicians, alleged informers and alleged criminals; 20 (16%) members or former members of republican paramilitary groups; 8 (6%) members or former members of loyalist paramilitary groups and 2 members of the Irish security forces.

PART 2: LOYALIST PARAMILITARY ORGANIZATIONS

Loyalist paramilitary organizations years active / operational	
Ulster Protestant Volunteers (UPV)	1966–1969
Ulster Volunteer Force (UVF)	1966-2007
Red Hand Commando (RHC)	1966–2007
Ulster Defence Association (UDA)	1971–2007
Ulster Freedom Fighters (UFF)	1971–2007
Ulster Resistance (UR)	1986 to ?
Loyalist Volunteer Force (LVF)	1996–2005
Orange Volunteers (OV)	1998 to present
Red Hand Defenders (RHD)	1998 to present

Republicans and nationalists were matched in their paramilitary activity during The Troubles by loyalists intent on championing Unionism, protecting Protestant communities and ruthlessly retaliating against republican violence.

Militant loyalism has its roots in 1912 and the introduction of the Home Rule Bill in the British parliament. Home Rule was anathema to Ulster Protestants, who shuddered at the prospect of a Dublin-based government led by Catholics and nationalists. Protestant communities in the Six Counties began organizing their own civilian militias which in 1913 combined to form the Ulster Volunteer Force (UVF). Under Edward Carson and James Craig, the UVF threatened civil war if a Home Rule dominated by Catholics was imposed on Ulster. In April 1914 the UVF smuggled around 20,000 German rifles and millions of rounds of ammunition into Northern Ireland. The Home Rule Bill was passed in May 1914 but the implementation of Home Rule was set aside due to the outbreak of the Great War in August. Instead of taking up arms against Dublin, thousands of Ulster Volunteers enlisted for military service in Europe. The UVF declined and was eventually demobilized in 1919. It was revived briefly during the Irish War of Independence (1920–22) to respond to IRA violence in

A troop of Ulster Volunteers.

Ulster. Many of its members went on to join the Ulster Special Constabulary (USC) or 'B Specials'.

Loyalists paramilitary groups came back together in the 1960s, in response to the civil rights movement and growing unrest in Northern Ireland. Two paramilitary groups were formed in 1966: the Ulster Protestant Volunteers (UPV) and the Ulster Volunteer Force (UVF). The UPV was a small Christian fundamentalist group led by the Reverend Ian Paisley, best remembered for bombing several power stations and water-supply facilities in March and April 1969, as a protest against the Unionist government's reformist policies. The UVF was formed in May 1966, fifty years after Easter Rising.

The modus operandi of loyalist paramilitaries was similar to the methods of the IRA and, as with the IRA, many of their victims were innocent civilians caught in the crossfire, or who just had the misfortune to be in the wrong place at the wrong time.

Ulster Defence Association

Recently declassified papers discovered by researchers from the Pat Finucane Centre in Derry show that there did indeed exist an unhealthy alliance between the state and loyalists in the early years of the conflict. The bloodiest year was 1972, when there was a bombing or a shooting every 40 minutes. At up to 50,000 strong, the largest loyalist paramilitary organization was the Ulster Defence Association. By the summer of 1972, with their masks, dark glasses and khaki fatigues, the UDA were strutting around Belfast, some members brandishing offensive weapons. Their message to the army

COLLUSION IS NOT AN ILLUSION

10 people from Ardoyne were murdered by weapons imported by the British Government from South Africa by their agent Brian Nelson in January 1988 until 1994

The consignment of weapons smuggled in by Nelson...... 200 AK47 rifles 90 Browning 9mm pistols 500 Grenades 30,000 Rounds of ammunition 1 Dozen RPG7 rocket launchers and warheads

IT IS STATE MURDER

Mural in the Ardoyne, north Belfast.

was: "You deal with the IRA or we will." ('Collusion Cut Both Ways in The Troubles,' John Ware in *Standpoint*, July/August 2015)

The UDA was notable for its women's units who assisted at roadblocks and were involved in local community work and for making up and delivering food parcels to UDA prisoners. The Sandy Row women's UDA unit was disbanded after the heinous 'romper room' punishment beating on July 24, 1974 which saw Ann Ogilby (32), a Protestant single mother, brutally murdered, her body found in a ditch five days later. Her crime: an affair with the husband of one of the unit's members. Ogilby was abducted and forced upstairs to the first floor of a disused bakery in Sandy Row converted into a UDA club. Two teenage girls, Henrietta Cowan and Christine Smith were ordered to give Ogilby a 'good rompering' and so she was punched, kicked, then battered to death with bricks and sticks all within earshot of Ogilby's six-year-old daughter. The post mortem revealed that twenty-four blows had been administered; the killing was condemned by UDA prisoners serving in the Maze Prison. The UDA 'romper rooms', named after a children's television programme, were hell holes where victims were beaten and tortured before being killed. The 'romper rooms' were in disused buildings, lock-up garages, warehouses, and rooms above pubs and drinking clubs.

The UDA was the largest loyalist paramilitary force in Northern Ireland. Established in September 1971 it was, for twenty-four years or so, engaged in defending Protestant loyalist areas in the fight against Irish republicanism, as spearheaded by the Provisional IRA. During the 1970s it was not uncommon to see uniformed UDA members patrolling their areas armed with batons and organizing marches and rallies. The paramilitary wing of the UDA went by the cover name the Ulster Freedom Fighters (UFF), to ensure that the UDA would not be proscribed by the British and Irish governments. Astonishingly the ploy worked. While the UFF was outlawed in November 1973, the UDA was allowed to operate until August 1992: an unbelievable example of long-term British government connivance with loyalist terrorist activity.

At its launch, Charles Harding Smith was leader, with former British soldier Davy Fogel as his second-in-command. Fogel used his invaluable military experience to train new recruits in military strategy and tactics, gun-handling and unarmed combat. Ironically, its first motto was *Cedenta Arma Togae* ('Law before violence'). This, in time, was replaced by *Quis Seperabit?* ('Who will separate us?'): patently not the British government.

Mural for North Down Ulster Freedom Fighters, Bloomfield estate, Bangor. (Photo by Keresaspa)

The UDA was nothing if not popular with around 40,000 members at its peak, most of whom were part-time. All told, the UDA/UFF was responsible for more than 400 deaths, with most of its victims being Catholic civilians killed at random and indiscriminately, in so-called retaliation for IRA attacks on Protestants. Most attacks were confined to Northern Ireland, but from 1972 the group organized bombings in the Republic. The UDA/UFF declared a ceasefire in 1994 and concluded its paramilitary activity in 2007.

The UDA brand of terrorism reached its nadir in the early 1990s through Johnny Adair's ruthless leadership of C Company, Lower Shankill 2nd Battalion; C Company's murder squad, led by Stephen McKeag, was infamous for its campaign of random murders of Catholic civilians. They were helped enormously by a group called Ulster Resistance set up by the Democratic Unionist Party, now in bed with the Conservative government, and by an arms shipment imported from Lebanon in 1988. The weapons included rocket launchers, 200 rifles, ninety pistols and over 400 grenades.

Allegations of collusion between the UDA and the British government—specifically that the British Army and RUC were feeding the UDA target lists of Irish republican activists—came to a head in 1992 when Brian Nelson, a prominent UDA member convicted of sectarian killings, came out as a British Army agent. Subsequently, UDA members have confirmed that they received intelligence files on republicans from British Army and RUC intelligence sources. A 1985 MI5 assessment reported that 85% of the UDA's "targeting material" came from the security forces. A "very senior RUC officer" was also suspected by MI5 of "assisting loyalist paramilitaries to procure arms". The UDA's five Belfast 'Brigade' areas were allegedly in contact with around a hundred police officers.

Of the high-profile UDA/UFF attacks, one of the most atrocious was the Greysteel Massacre in October 1993 when three men wearing blue boiler suits and balaclavas opened fire indiscriminately in the Rising Sun restaurant in the predominantly Catholic village of Greysteel, County Derry, as seventy people were celebrating Halloween. One of the killers, Stephen Irwin, shouted "Trick or treat!" as he opened fire with a Vz. 58 assault rifle on the packed crowd in the lounge. He emptied his magazine, reloaded and continued shooting. Eight people, including six Catholics and two Protestants, were killed and nineteen wounded. Apparently, the gunmen were laughing as they made their escape in an Opel Kadett: the car's wing mirror was clipped by a police car speeding towards the scene.

A February 16, 2006 report in *The Guardian* stated: "Torrens Knight, 36, was part of Ulster Freedom Fighters gang which sprayed a Co. Derry pub with bullets, killing eight people and injuring 19, in the 'trick or treat' massacre on Halloween night 1993. Now Nuala O'Loan, the Northern Ireland police ombudsman, is investigating allegations that Knight, said to have become a born-again Christian while in jail, was a police informant. The ombudsman's team is also investigating claims that a gun later used in the Greysteel murders was moved before police could recover it. Informed sources told the Press Association in Belfast that cash was lodged in a bank account set up for Knight, and staff told he was employed by a Scottish firm as an engineer on a £50,000-a-year salary. But the arrangement ended after two payments—it is unclear just how much money Knight may have received. The ombudsman's office has been told anglers stumbled on high-powered rifles, belonging to the UFF, after the Castlerock shootings but police failed to find them after a search along the Agivey river. It has been alleged that a Special Branch officer moved the guns to protect Knight's identity. The Police Service of Northern Ireland has refused to comment on the claims."

The UFF claimed the attack was in retaliation to the IRA's Shankill Road bombing, which had killed nine people seven days earlier. On October 23, 1993, an IRA bomb had blown up prematurely as the bombers carried it into a chip shop on the Shankill Road. The intended target was a meeting of UDA leaders, including brigadier Johnny Adair, which was scheduled to take place in a room above the shop; however, unknown to the IRA, the meeting was rescheduled and eight Protestant civilians, a UDA member and one of the IRA bombers were killed.

Other UDA revenge attacks for Shankill Road included the murder of a Catholic delivery driver and the shooting dead of another two Catholic civilians and wounding five more in an attack at the Council Depot at Kennedy Way, Belfast.

In March 1988 the Milltown Cemetery killings occurred in the middle of the funeral of three Provisional IRA volunteers killed in Gibraltar by the SAS. A UDA volunteer and maverick, Michael Stone, attacked the crowds of thousands of mourners, who included Sinn Féin's Gerry Adams and Martin McGuinness. He was throwing seven-second-delay hand grenades and shooting pistols as the second coffin—that of Sean Savage—was about to be lowered into the ground to the bagpipers' skirl of *The Minstrel Boy*. Shooting and lobbing grenades all the while, he was pursued by a crowd of incensed mourners up towards the M1 motorway a quarter of a mile away where he was caught and beaten up, only to be rescued and arrested by the police. Stone killed three men and wounded more than sixty in his attack; among the injured was a pregnant mother of four, a seventy-two-year-old grandmother and a ten-year-old boy. The incident was captured on TV and beamed around the world.

The New York Times of March 17, 1988: "The grieving families back on the hill arose and completed the burials amid the emotional uproar even as the bodies of the newly slain were carried off bloodied in one of the waiting hearses. 'God, we can't even bury the dead in peace,' one woman declared, her Belfast lilt hard-edged with terror."

Writing in the March 19 edition of *The Irish Times*, Kevin Myers, a staunch opponent of republican paramilitary violence, wrote: "Unarmed young men charged against the man hurling grenades and firing an automatic pistol ... The young men stalking their quarry repeatedly came under fire; they were repeatedly bombed; they repeatedly advanced. Indeed this was not simply bravery; this was a heroism which in other circumstances, I have no doubt, would have won the highest military decorations."

The fallout from the attack caused consternation. The UDA and the Ulster Volunteer Force (UVF) both denied responsibility. The leader of the UDA West Belfast Brigade, Tommy Lyttle, tried to distance the UDA from Stone and said that Stone was a lone, rogue agent acting independently without orders, although he did not condemn the attack. UDA member Sammy Duddy confirmed the confusion when, as quoted by Ian Wood, he maintained: "After Milltown, two UDA brigadiers from two Belfast battalions telephoned the IRA to say they didn't know Michael Stone ... But Michael was UDA, he was a travelling gunman who went after the IRA and republicans and he needed no authority for that because that was his job. Those two brigadiers were scared in case the IRA would retaliate against them ... so they disclaimed Michael, one of our best operators."

This all came in the wake of a crucial policy change by the British government relating to operational procedure at paramilitary funerals. Republicans and church leaders had been complaining for years about heavy-handed policing of IRA funerals, which had often led to violence. So, the British Army and the RUC prudently decided to take a step back at the funerals of 'The Gibraltar Three'.

Sinn Féin, according to Stair na hÉireann, were among those who "claimed that there must have been collusion with the security forces, because only a small number of people knew in advance of the reduced police presence at the funerals". Stone later said that he had been given assurances that British soldiers and RUC officers would not be deployed in the graveyard and that he had inside information about British Army and RUC movements that day. He added that he was "given his pick of weapons from an Ulster Resistance cache at a secret location outside Belfast" and was "driven back into the city by a member of the RUC". Some journalists maintain that the weapons he used were issued to him on the orders of UDA intelligence chief Brian Nelson, who was later uncovered as an undercover agent of the British Army's Force Research Unit (FRU). A further consequence of Stone's actions was the 'Corporals Killings' in which, three days later, two Det corporals stumbled into the funeral of one of Stone's victims, Caoimhín Mac Brádaigh, and were savagely murdered, again live on TV.

1992 had started badly: the UDA welcomed in the new year on January 9 when a Lisburn-based UDA unit shot dead Catholic civilian Phillip Campbell at work nearby.

The unit followed this up by killing another Catholic civilian, Paul Moran and then a few days later members of the UDA West Belfast Brigade shot taxi driver Paddy Clarke dead at his north Belfast home. However, the UDA decided that, while this piecemeal murder was all well and good, something more extravagant was required to get their message across: Sean Graham's bookmaker's shop with its Catholic clientele near the UDA stronghold of the Annadale Flats fitted the bill nicely.

February 5, 1992 was just another ordinary, if foggy, day in Sean Graham's bookmaker's shop on the Lower Ormeau Road in nationalist Belfast until, that is, members of the UDA in the guise of UFF burst in and opened fire. At 2.20 p.m. two men, dressed in boiler suits and balaclavas, emerged from a car parked on University Avenue facing the bookmaker's and crossed the Ormeau Road to the shop. One was armed with a Vz.58 Czechoslovak assault rifle and the other with a 9mm pistol. They entered the shop—where there were fifteen customers—and opened fire, firing forty-four rounds in all. The eldest victim was Jack Duffin (66), the youngest James Kennedy (15). Four died there in the shop but Kennedy survived until he reached the hospital. Kennedy's mother Kathleen died two years later after becoming a recluse. Her husband, James (Sr.), blamed his wife's death on the shooting by poignantly claiming that "the bullets that killed James didn't just travel in distance, they travelled in time. Some of those bullets never stopped travelling." The UDA claimed responsibility saying that the shooting was in retaliation for the Teebane bombing, perpetrated by the Provisional IRA nearly three weeks before.

In November 1992 another bookmaker's in another Catholic part of town was the scene of another massacre. Two UDA men entered the shop on the Oldpark Road in the republican Bone area very close to the peace line with the loyalist lower Oldpark. Allegedly Stephen McKeag opened fire on the customers with a Vz. 58 assault rifle while another volunteer threw a Soviet-made fragmentation grenade, shouting, Youse deserve it, youse Fenian bastards!" Two Catholics, Francis Burns (52) and Peter Orderly (47) died instantly and a third, John Lovett (72), died of his injuries in hospital the following day. Lovett was a Second World War veteran who had survived torture in a Japanese camp as an RAF prisoner of war; amidst the carnage he took control and kept shouting, "Keep your calm." Protestants also frequented the betting shop, and one who nearly died was among the several others injured in the attack. The murders were reportedly celebrated by "a raucous celebration in a loyalist club in south Belfast with Johnny Adair occupying centre stage".

On March 25, 1993 UDA members shot dead three Catholic civilians and a Provisional Irish Republican Army volunteer as they arrived for work in their van in Castlerock, County Derry. Another was wounded. The five men were builders who had been renovating houses in the Gortree Park housing estate for some months.

Two or more gunmen jumped out of another van and opened fire, killing three of the builders.

In 1996, on the same day as the Hillcrest Bar bombing by the Glenanne Gang, Catholic teacher John Donnelly was enjoying a drink in the Cregagh Inn on Woodstock Road when one of his former students pointed him out as a Catholic; UDA members who happened to be in the pub forced him outside in full view of the customers and stabbed him to death.

According to Sutton the UDA/UFF was responsible for at least 260 killings, and lists a further 256 loyalist killings that have not yet been attributed to a particular group. According to *Lost Lives* (2006), it was responsible for 431 killings. The CAIN database records that there were 91 UDA members and four former members killed in the conflict. Of those killed by the UDA/UFF: 209 (80%) were civilians, twelve of whom were civilian political activists; 11 (4%) were members or former members of republican paramilitary groups; 37 (14%) were members or former members of loyalist paramilitary groups; 3 (1%) were members of the British security forces

THE TORIES ARE FORMING A COALITION WITH A PARTY [THE DUP] BACKED BY TERRORISTS

The UDA is a violent loyalist paramilitary group, which is still active today. Just weeks ago, it murdered a man in broad daylight in Northern Ireland—he was shot dead in a Sainsbury's car park in front of horrified shoppers and his three-year-old son ... Most striking about the Conservatives' new stablemates is that after running a campaign based on fearmongering and whipping up false hysteria about Jeremy Corbyn and his alleged IRA sympathies, the Conservatives will enter government with the DUP, which is backed by the Ulster Defence Association (UDA). The UDA is less known in England than the IRA, largely because they killed Northern Irish Catholics during The Troubles, which didn't make the news as often as the killing of English people or security personnel ... There is no suggestion that the DUP actively sought the endorsement from the group or that it in turn supports the UDA. However, concerns were further fuelled when it emerged that the DUP's leader Arlene Foster met with the UDA's chief during the election campaign, just 48 hours after the murder of a local man in a supermarket car park.

Siobhan Fenton, *The Independent*, Friday, June 9, 2017

Ulster Volunteer Force

On May 24, 1966, the Ulster Volunteer Force issued this uncompromising statement: "From this day, we declare war against the Irish Republican Army and its splinter groups. Known IRA men will be executed mercilessly and without hesitation. Less extreme measures will be taken against anyone sheltering or helping them, but if they persist in giving them aid, then more extreme methods will be adopted ... we solemnly warn the authorities to make no more speeches of appeasement. We are heavily armed Protestants dedicated to this cause."

The previous month loyalists led by Ian Paisley set up the Ulster Constitution Defence Committee (UCDC) and established a paramilitary wing under the name of the Ulster Protestant Volunteers (UPV). The objective was to counter any upsurge in IRA activity in the North, emasculate the civil rights movement and depose Terence O'Neill, prime minister of Northern Ireland. O'Neill was a unionist but he was seen by hard-line loyalists as being too lenient on the civil rights movement—so he had to go.

Simultaneously, the Ulster Volunteer Force (UVF) emerged from the Shankill area of Belfast led by Gusty Spence, a former British soldier who served with the Royal Ulster Rifles. Their operational base was the Standard Bar, a pub on the Shankill Road frequented by Spence and his comrades. Many of the UVF were also members of the UCDC and UPV. UVF violence began in April 1966 when members petrol-bombed Catholic homes, schools and businesses. A firebomb killed an innocent elderly Protestant widow, Matilda Gould, who lived next door to the pub that was targeted. On May 27 the UVF shot dead a Catholic civilian, John Scullion; in June it executed three Catholic civilians as they left a pub, killing a young Catholic from the Republic, Peter Ward. The UVF was duly proscribed; Spence and others were arrested. Spence, however, was by now something of a legend: his involvement in the murder campaign is said to have inspired Michael Stone and other radicals.

Like the UDA, the UVF pledged to fight Irish republicanism—particularly as it manifested in the IRA—and to maintain Northern Ireland as part of the United Kingdom. It was responsible for more than 500 deaths, more than two-thirds of its victims being Catholic civilians usually killed at random. The, somewhat naïve, hope was that by terrorizing the Catholic community and killing more and more Catholics, the IRA would give up its struggle. Responsibility for many of the UVF attacks was claimed using the cover name Protestant Action Force (PAF), from 1974, signing off their statements with the pseudonym Captain William Johnston. They were nothing if not prolific: no-warning pub bombings were a speciality and toward the end of 1973, the UVF detonated more bombs than the UDA and IRA put together. Up until the temporary November ceasefire the UVF had claimed responsibility for over

UVF mural in Shankill Road, Belfast. (Photo by E. Asterion)

200 explosions that year. However, from 1977 bombs almost disappeared from the UVF's armoury due to a lack of explosives and bomb-makers only to make a return in the early 1990s when it took possession of a stash of the mining explosive Powergel, an explosive used in mining.

As noted, the new UVF hoped to gain kudos from its association with the Ulster Volunteers, a unionist militia founded in 1912 to prevent Home Rule for Ireland, then part of the United Kingdom, by a Catholic-majority parliament in Dublin. The Ulster Volunteers power base was the then northern province of Ulster. The militias were organized into the Ulster Volunteer Force (UVF) in 1913. In response, the Irish nationalists formed a rival militia, the Irish Volunteers, to promote Home Rule. The Great War ensured that the Home Rule crisis was shelved. Many UVF members enlisted with the British Army's 36th (Ulster) Division.

In furtherance of their strategy to depose Terence O'Neill in 1969 UVF and UPV members bombed water and electricity installations in Northern Ireland, laying the blame on the IRA who were dormant at the time, and on the civil rights movement. Much of Belfast was left without power and water; British troops were deployed to guard installations; on April 28 O'Neill resigned as prime minister.

When the Hunt Committee, set up after the Derry riots, published its report on October 12, recommending that the RUC become an unarmed force and the B Specials be stood down, the loyalists took to the streets and during violence in the Shankill

The early UVF practising standing-position rifle shooting in about 1915.

UVF members shot dead RUC officer Victor Arbuckle, the first RUC officer to be killed during The Troubles. Between October and December 1969, the UVF carried out bombings in the Republic of Ireland including the RTÉ Television Centre in Dublin. Further acts of terrorism followed when UVF and UPV member Thomas McDowell was killed by the bomb he was planting at Ballyshannon power station in protest against the Irish Army units "still massed on the border in County Donegal". In December, the UVF exploded a car bomb at the Garda central detective bureau and telephone exchange headquarters in Dublin.

The UVF economic campaign against nationalists continued into 1970 to "remove republican elements from loyalist areas" and stop them "reaping financial benefit there from". During that year (1970), forty-two Catholic-owned licensed premises in Protestant areas were bombed; Catholic churches were attacked and the UVF targeted critics of militant loyalism: bomb attacks were made on the homes of MPs Austin Currie, Sheelagh Murnaghan, Richard Ferguson and Anne Dickson. The attacks in the Republic of Ireland continued apace with bombings of the Dublin–Belfast railway line, an electricity substation, a radio mast and Irish nationalist monuments.

But it was in 1971 that the UDF joined the exclusive club of murder squads, in response to increased IRA action against the British Army and RUC. The first British soldier to be killed by the Provisional IRA died in February 1971. Tit-for-tat pub bombings began in Belfast, reaching a peak on December 4 with the UVF bombing of McGurk's Bar, a Catholic-owned pub in Belfast. Fifteen Catholic civilians were killed—including two children—and seventeen wounded in the explosion which collapsed the bar, an atrocity that was the UVF's deadliest attack in Northern Ireland, and the bloodiest attack in Belfast during The Troubles.

Despite overwhelming evidence to the contrary, the British security forces tried to shift the blame away from loyalists onto nationalists by asserting that the bomb had exploded prematurely while being handled in the bar by members of the IRA. The RUC supported this fake news, hindering the investigation as a consequence. Tit-for-tat bombings and shootings by loyalists and republicans were the outcome, making 1972 the bloodiest year of the conflict.

McGurk's Bar—also known as the Tramore Bar—was a two-storey public house on the corner of North Queen Street and Great George's Street, in the New Lodge area, north Belfast, a predominantly nationalist and Catholic part of the city. The pub was owned by Patrick and Philomena McGurk, who lived on the upper floor with their four children.

In the weeks leading up to the outrage there had been some seventy bombings in which approximately thirty people were killed. Tensions increased on December 2 when all that three high-profile republican prisoners—Martin Meehan, Anthony 'Dutch' Doherty and Hugh McCann—had to do to escape was simply scale the wall of Crumlin Road jail and jump down to freedom. The prison was near McGurk's, and the escape naturally led to a marked increase in security by the RUC and British Army. Ominously, though, eyewitnesses have stated that the checkpoints around McGurk's were disabled just an hour before the attack. Of the night of the bombing the *Belfast Telegraph* reported: "In a massive clamp-down operation, hundreds of troops today saturated Belfast's city centre ... in an effort to prevent a repetition of last Saturday's IRA terror campaign ... More than 4,000 men in nine regiments are stationed in and around Belfast, and today each regiment was told to keep a lookout for trouble in its own area ... All this was in addition to the massive search which has been mounted for the three IRA jail breakers. Road blocks on all roads leading into and out of the city are being manned round the clock."

The inexplicability of the military situation is well summed up by Wayback Machine: "Witnesses recall that there were cordons and searches at every turn and yet it was in this area that a loyalist death squad felt confident to linger and act. The military on this one major road had somehow vanished to allow a carload of men with a 30–50lb bomb on the backseat into their target zone." (*See also* http://mcgurks-bar.com/collusion)

McGurk's was unlucky for more than the obvious reason. On the evening of Saturday, December 4, 1971, a four-man UVF team was uncompromisingly ordered to bomb 'a pub' on North Queen Street and not to bother coming back until and unless the job was done. The original target had not been McGurk's, but a pub nearby called The Gem, known to have close links with the Official IRA. The 50-pound bomb was wrapped up to make a brown parcel and driven to The Gem at about 7.30 p.m. However, the bombers were unable to get in due to the presence of security guards outside. After an hour, they made the fateful decision to drive up the road to McGurk's and at about 8.45 p.m., left the bomb in the pub porch on Great George's Street; the bomb exploded as they sped off. The job was done. According to the *Belfast Telegraph* of April 20, 2013, "those who were not crushed or suffocated were horrifically burned when shattered gas mains burst into flames beneath the rubble".

Philomena McGurk was one of the casualties, Maria McGurk, her twelve-year-old daughter, another. Patrick McGurk and his three sons were seriously injured. After the attack, the bereaved father appeared on television calling for no retaliation: "It doesn't matter who planted the bomb. What's done can't be undone. I've been trying to keep bitterness out of it."

Apart from the belief that the bomb had had been planted by loyalists, there was a contrived suggestion that it had exploded prematurely while being prepared by IRA members inside the pub or that it had exploded prematurely while in transit, an IRA member having left it in the pub to be collected by another IRA member and, alternatively, that the bomb had been planted to stoke a feud between the Provisional IRA and Official IRA. Later, British intelligence had to deny that the pub had IRA connections.

The UVF statement in the *Belfast Telegraph* ran as follows: "We [the Empire Loyalists] accept responsibility for the destruction of McGurk's pub. We placed 30lb of new explosives outside the pub because we had proved beyond doubt that meetings of IRA Provisionals and Officials were held there."

Meanwhile on pages 27 and 28 of the Police Ombudsman's Report: "A scrap of paper carelessly left by a UDF member in a nearby telephone box held further revealing information; while it alluded to collusion, it also complicated the issue yet further: 'We the Empire Loyalists wish to state that we did not destroy McGurk's public house as an act of retaliation ... Furthermore we do not require the forensic experts of the Army to cover up for us ... We shall not issue any further statements until we exterminate another rebel stronghold.'"

Further confusion came with a letter sent to the RUC claiming that the UVF blew up the pub to destroy an IRA meeting due to take place there, claiming that two UVF members entered the pub, had a drink and asked the barman to mind a package while they "ran an errand". However, the police report confirms that no strangers were reported in the pub and nobody had left a package. Three other unsigned letters sent to the RUC claimed it was an IRA bomb in transit and that two IRA members were killed.

The RUC persisted with their friendly-fire conclusion, denying any collusion. Relatives questioned why the bomb could have been planted despite the heavy security presence and why the security forces assisted the bombers by suddenly removing checkpoints. A former UVF member, 'John Black', has claimed in his 2009 book *Killing For Britain* that the Military Reaction Force or Military Reconnaissance Force (MRF) set up the bombing and assisted the bombers, blaming it on the Provisional IRA with the intention of fomenting a feud between the two IRA factions, and thus deflecting them from their campaign against British forces. The claim may be substantiated by the fact that one of the getaway team deserted and fled his comrades: no loyalist was ever punished for this treachery, as might be

A mocked-up bar front on the spot where the actual McGurk's Bar was destroyed by a bomb in 1971, corner of Great George's Street and North Queen Street, Belfast. (Photo by Keresaspa)

expected, leading to the suggestion that the gang member was a member of British intelligence.

Immediately after the outrage, the British swung into action: the recently formed Psychological Operations (PsyOps) section based at Belfast's Palace Barracks and GHQ Lisburn—the Information Research Department—started pedalling the lie that the bomb was 'an IRA own-goal'. The campaign to fan the flames of internecine IRA war was well under way. The minutes of a secret military briefing (ref. MG/71/1338 55/20/6) on December 14, 1971, discussed how the lie was to be further propagated at governmental level: "Findings which indicated that that the explosion in the McGurk's Bar had been the result of a bomb in the bar should be publicized, possibly by means of a written parliamentary question."

The Guardian added to the propaganda when on December 24, 1971 it reported: "Security men and forensic scientists have finished the grisly investigation of the explosion in Paddy McGurk's Bar ... If they are to be believed—and in this case they probably are—this figure will have to be revised upwards. They claim to have established that five men were standing round the bomb when it went off inside the crowded bar in North Queen Street. All five were blown to pieces. The scientists have been able to identify one of them as a senior IRA man who was an expert on explosives and was on the government's wanted list. Of all the conflicting theories about the explosion, the security men are now convinced that the bar was a transfer point in the IRA chain between the makers and the planters of the bomb. Something went wrong and the bomb exploded."

This, however, does not chime with Dr Robert Alan Hall's report of February 11, 1972: he was the forensic scientist in charge of the case and concluded that "the combined findings, including the pathology reports, did not support the theory that a group of men were standing over or near the bomb. Tests for shrapnel or parts of the detonating device upon the victims' clothing proved negative. No debris at all from an explosive device was found upon any of the victims' clothing. In fact those nearest to the seat of the blast had splinter injuries which indicated that furniture, probably a door, was in between them and the bomb when it exploded." Hall concluded that the explosion "had occurred at or about the entrance door from the porch leading off Great Georges Street".

Changes to the official line eventually took place in July 2009 when a Director of Operations Brief document prepared for the General Officer Commanding the British forces in the north of Ireland at the time, Lieutenant-General Sir Harry Tuzo, clearly shows that the Army Technical Officer on the scene minutes after the explosion believed, in his expert opinion, the bomb "to have been planted *outside* the pub". This directly challenges the official Palace Barracks/RUC version of events which clearly has more than a whiff of collusion and cover-up about it.

Put simply, if the government of Northern Ireland under Brian Faulkner admitted that loyalists carried out the butchery at McGurk's, their assertion to the Westminster government that loyalists posed "no serious threat" would be untenable. Add to this the crescendo in insurgency violence since August 1971, then Whitehall could do no other than admit that internment without trial was an unmitigated failure and a disaster of the first order.

In December 2016 at an information tribunal in London, it was revealed that key evidence was contained in a high-level Headquarters Northern Ireland Commander's diary. This expert opinion supported all of the evidence including, crucially, an eyewitness who saw the bombers plant the bomb in the porch and flee; the evidence was suppressed as it flew in the face of the lies which the police created and promulgated. Other vital evidence was withheld during closed sessions of the information tribunal. Most significantly, a barrister representing the Ministry of Defence was forced to admit that the department was withholding information to protect the identity of an agent/informer.

It was not until December 15, 2017, however, that more of the truth came out: victims and survivors of the McGurk's Bar atrocity learned that alleged PSNI agent and UVF commander Gary Haggarty passed information to his handlers about the massacre, information to which the Police Ombudsman's office was privy. Neither the Police Service of Northern Ireland nor the Police Ombudsman's office divulged this information to the families, and neither organization disclosed this in any of its investigations into the McGurk's Bar Massacre even though this information could have been significant and germane to their investigations.

Like the fledgling UDA, the UVF saw in the 1972 new year by instigating a campaign of gun attacks on random Catholic civilians and exploding car bombs in Catholic pubs. On October 23, 1972, the UVF raided King's Park camp, a UDR/Territorial Army depot in Lurgan from which they stole a large cache of weapons and ammunition including L1A1 Self-Loading Rifles, Browning pistols, and Sterling submachine guns. Twenty tons of ammonium nitrate—a high-nitrogen fertilizer and a widely used bulk industrial explosive—were also stolen from Belfast docks. South of the border, UVF volunteers killed five civilians when it detonated three car bombs in Dublin and one in Belturbet, a town in County Cavan, during December 1972 and January 1973. In May 1974, it exacerbated the two-week Ulster Workers' Council strike, a general strike in protest against the Sunningdale Agreement, blocking roads, intimidating workers, and closing down any businesses that opened.

On May 17, two UVF units from the Belfast and Mid-Ulster brigades detonated four car bombs in Dublin and Monaghan. Crucially, in April, the British government had lifted the UVF's status as a proscribed organization. At 1727 all was normal, just another hectic, hurried commute home; at 1728 all that changed: the carnage that was unleashed by the four bombs abruptly ended the lives of thirty-three innocent people and changed things irrevocably for hundreds of physically injured, grieving and psychologically scarred victims.

May 17, 1974 was the day that, even by the horrific standards set by the atrocities of The Troubles thus far, the carnage excelled with four coordinated bombings in Dublin and Monaghan; no warnings were given. This, the deadliest attack in the Republic's history, saw three bombs explode in Dublin during evening rush hour and a fourth explode in Monaghan, just south of the border, almost ninety minutes later. Between them, the UVF bombs indiscriminately slaughtered thirty-three innocent civilians and a full-term unborn child, injuring two hundred and fifty-eight. The ages of the dead ranged from five months to eighty years; most of the victims were young female civil service office workers, commuters and shoppers. An entire family from central Dublin was killed. Two of the victims were from overseas: an Italian man, and a French Jewish woman whose family had survived the Holocaust. The buses were on strike that day in Dublin which meant that the pavements and

Members of the public tend to the injured following the detonation of the bomb on Talbot Street in Dublin in May 1974. (Photo by Tom Lawlor)

roads were busier than usual. The bombs impacted on more people than would have been normal and the emergency services had major problems reaching the bomb scenes.

Dublin bomb number one exploded at about 1728 on Parnell Street, near the junction with Marlborough Street in a parking bay outside the Welcome Inn pub and Barry's supermarket at 93 and 91 Parnell Street respectively; petrol pumps were close by. The car in which the bomb had been placed was a metallic green 1970 Hillman Avenger, registration number DIA 4063, hijacked in Belfast that morning. Ten people were killed in this explosion, including two young girls and their parents, and a Great War veteran.

Bomb number two detonated at about 1730 on Talbot Street, near the intersection with Lower Gardiner Street. Talbot Street is the main route from the city centre to Connolly railway station to which hundreds were flocking. The bomb car was a metallic blue Ford Escort (1385 WZ) parked at 18 Talbot Street opposite Guiney's department store and stolen that morning in the Docks area of Belfast. Twelve people were killed outright, and another two died later. Thirteen of the fourteen victims were women, one of whom was nine months pregnant. One young woman was decapitated—her sex was only determined by the brown platform boots she was wearing. Others lost limbs and a man was impaled through the abdomen with an iron bar. Some victims were hurled through shop windows. Several bodies lay in the street for half an hour as ambulances struggled to get through traffic jams. Passersby covered the bodies of the victims with newspapers.

Bomb number three went off at about 1732 on South Leinster Street, near Trinity College. Two women were killed. The bomb car was a blue Austin 1800 (HOI 2487) hijacked in Belfast that morning from a taxi company. Trinity College dental students rushed to the scene to give first aid to the injured.

The 150-pound Monaghan bomb exploded ninety minutes later, at about 1858 in Monaghan town centre. The car, a green 1966 Hillman Minx (6583 OZ) had been stolen from a Portadown car park a few hours before. As in Dublin, no warning was given. The explosion killed five people outright while two more died in the following weeks. Forensic analysis suggested that the bomb had been in a beer barrel or similar container. The Monaghan bombing was probably a 'supporting attack', a diversion to draw security forces away from the border to enable the Dublin bombers to return to Northern Ireland.

There have been no charges related to the bombings. Pressure exerted by the victims' families led to an Irish government inquiry under Justice Henry Barron. His 2003 report criticised the Garda Síochána's investigation and said the investigators

The aftermath of the bomb in Monaghan town.

stopped their work too soon. Criticism was also levelled at the Fine Gael/Labour government for its tepid reaction and obvious lack of interest in the bombings. Again, as with the horror at McGurk's, allegations of British government collusion with the UDF were rife including participation by members of the notorious Glenanne gang; some of these allegations originate from former members of the security forces. Justice Barron's inquiry was seriously hampered by the British government's persistent refusal to release key documents. The victims' families, for their part, have doggedly campaigned for the British government to release these papers.

Sammy Smyth, then press officer of both the UDA and the Ulster Workers' Council (UWC) Strike Committee, said at the time, "I am very happy about the bombings in Dublin. There is a war with the Free State and now we are laughing at them." However, neither the UDA nor UVF admitted responsibility immediately. A Captain Craig telephoned the *Irish News* and *The Irish Times*, claiming responsibility for the bombings on behalf of the Red Hand Brigade, a UVF cover name.

In 1993 the UVF finally claimed responsibility for the bombings, asserting that they acted alone. This was following Yorkshire Television's documentary about the bombings, *Hidden Hand: The Forgotten Massacre* that named the UVF as the murderers, and which alleged that British security forces were implicated in the atrocity. The documentary also implicated a number of UVF members including Billy Hanna (a sergeant in the UDR), Robert McConnell (a UDR corporal), Harris Boyle (another UDR soldier), and a loyalist referred to as 'The Jackal', a former UDR soldier Robin Jackson. The documentary alleged that all of these men were working as agents for the British Intelligence Corps and RUC Special Branch. The documentary also suggested that British Army captain Robert Nairac, an operative in the covert Det, the Special Reconnaissance Unit/14 Intelligence Company, might have been involved. The documentary stated: "We have evidence from police, military and loyalist sources which confirms ... that in May 1974, he was meeting with these paramilitaries, supplying them with arms and helping them plan acts of terrorism." In a rare show of unity, a number of bomb disposal and munitions experts from the British Army, the Garda and the Irish army all agreed that the bombs were too sophisticated for the UVF and that it could not have mounted the attack without practical and expert help from the security forces. Allegations concerning the existence of a covert British Army unit based at Castledillon were considered, as well as alleged links between that unit and loyalist paramilitaries. It was shown that Merlyn Rees, the former secretary of state, knew about the unit.

It was further suggested that a significant element within the security forces supported a military solution to The Troubles, rather than the political solution championed by Merlyn Rees, the British Labour government's Northern Ireland secretary who believed that his polices in 1974 had been undermined by a faction in British Army Intelligence, the inference being that the bombings were intended to wreck the Sunningdale Agreement and to force both governments take a stronger line against the IRA. The Irish parliament's Joint Committee on Justice called the bombings an act of "international terrorism" involving the British security forces. Both the UVF and the British government have denied the claims.

Unbelievable as it may sound, things got even worse with the UVF when, in 1974, hard-line members staged a coup and took over the brigade staff. The outcome was a toxic increase in sectarian killings and internecine feuding with the UDA and within the UVF itself. One of the UVF Mid-Ulster Brigade attacks at the time was the Miami Showband killings of July 31, 1975 when three members of the showband were murdered; they had been stopped at a bogus British Army checkpoint outside Newry in County Down.

Colin Wills, writing in 1999 in the *Sunday Mirror*, called the Miami Showband attack "one of the worst atrocities in the 30-year history of The Troubles". Frank McNally, writing in the *The Irish Times*, described the massacre as "an incident that encapsulated all the madness of the time".

This attack by the UVF took place on the A1 at Buskhill in County Down. The band was travelling home to Dublin after 2 a.m. after a gig in Banbridge. Halfway to Newry, their minibus was halted at what appeared to be a military checkpoint where

The Miami Showband: from this to this in a few terrifying minutes.

gunmen dressed in British Army uniforms ordered the band to line up by the road-side with their hands on their heads. More uniformed men emerged from the shadows making about ten gunmen in all. At least four of them were serving soldiers in the Ulster Defence Regiment; all were members of the UVF. It was at this point that a soldier identified by survivors as unmistakeably British, probably Det operative Robert Nairac, arrived on the scene.

The plan was to explode the bomb when the van resumed its journey, murdering the band and framing them as IRA bomb-smugglers. While two of the gunmen were surreptitiously concealing a ten-pound time bomb in the rear of the mini-bus, it exploded and killed them. Botched soldering on the timer clock caused the device to explode prematurely, blowing the minibus apart and killing two of the 'soldiers' instantly. They were both decapitated and their bodies dismembered and burned beyond recognition. The only identifiable body part from the bombers was a severed arm belonging to Wesley Somerville. It was found hundred yards from the site with a 'UVF Portadown' tattoo on it. The remaining gunmen opened fire on the band members who had all been knocked down into the field below the road by the force of the blast. Three of the musicians were killed: lead singer Fran O'Toole, trumpeter Brian McCoy, and guitarist Tony Geraghty. McCoy was shot in the back by nine rounds from a 9mm Luger pistol. O'Toole tried to flee but was machine-gunned twenty-two times, mostly in the face, as he lay on the ground. Geraghty also attempted to escape but was shot at least four times in the back of the head and back. Both men had begged for their lives before they were shot. Stephen Travers was seriously wounded by a dum-dum bullet but survived by pretending to be dead. Des McAlea was hit by the minibus door when it was blown off in the explosion, but was not badly wounded and lay hidden in thick undergrowth, undetected by the gunmen. He also survived and hitched a lift to the RUC barracks in Newry.

Two serving British soldiers and one former British soldier were later found guilty of the murders and were handed down life sentences. The murderers belonged to the Glenanne gang, a motley, clandestine alliance of loyalist militants, rogue police officers and British soldiers. It is alleged that British military intelligence agents were also involved. According to former Intelligence Corps agent Captain Fred Holroyd, the killings were organized by Det officer Robert Nairac, together with the UVF's Mid-Ulster Brigade and its commander Robin 'The Jackal' Jackson, linked to the attack by fingerprints.

Bad as the massacre was, the blow it did to Northern Ireland's live music scene, which had brought young Catholics and Protestants together, made it even more devastating. The 1975 Miami Showband line-up comprised four Catholics and two Protestants. According to *The Irish Times*, from the 1950s to the 1970s, as many as 700 bands travelled to venues all over Ireland every night.

Allegedly, the Provisional IRA's attack on the loyalist Bayardo Bar in the Shankill Road in mid-August was in retaliation for the Miami Showband ambush. Four Protestant civilians, two men and two women, and UVF member Hugh Harris were killed in the attack. Two days later, Portadown disc jockey Norman 'Mooch' Kerr (28) was murdered by the IRA as he packed away his equipment after a gig at the Camrick Bar in Armagh. Kerr was a close friend of Harris Boyle's, one of the UVF blown up in the van. The IRA killed him because of an alleged association with British Army officer and member of Det, 14th Intelligence Company, Captain Robert Nairac. Kerr's stolen diary gave him away.

Between 1975 and 1982, a unit of the UVF frighteningly nicknamed the Shankill Butchers took centre stage when they carried out a campaign of murders of Catholic civilians. Six of the twenty-three victims were abducted indiscriminately, beaten and tortured before having their throats hacked with a butcher's knife. Hatchets were also used. Six Protestants with whom the butchers had personal disputes also met their fate at their hands, as did two other Protestants mistaken for Catholics. When the majority of the gang were eventually caught, in February 1979, they received the longest combined prison sentences in UK legal history: eleven men were convicted of a total of nineteen murders, and forty-two life sentences were handed out. The judge described their "catalogue of horror" as "a lasting monument to blind sectarian bigotry". Head butcher was Lenny Murphy, an inveterate bully and career thug, shot dead by the IRA in a blizzard of over twenty bullets in November 1982, four months after being released from the Maze Prison.

The instruments of death and torture—large knives and meat-cleavers—were stolen by William Moore, one of the gang leaders, from the meat-processing factory where he used to work. The sheer randomness of the attacks, let alone the brutality, was chilling in itself. On the night of November 24/25, 1975 Francis Crossen (34), a Catholic father of two, just happened to be walking toward the city centre at about 12.40 a.m. when four of the Butchers, in one of the gang's taxis, pulled alongside Crossen. Murphy leaped out and hit the man with a wheel brace before dragging him into the taxi where he was savagely beaten and glassed. Off Wimbledon Street Crossen was dragged into an alleyway where Murphy cut his throat almost through to the spine with a butcher's knife. A relative of Crossen's said that the family was unable to have an open coffin at his wake because the body was so badly mutilated.

Another Catholic butchered by the gang was Cornelius 'Con' Neeson (49), attacked with a hatchet on the Cliftonville Road late on August 1, 1976. In 1994 one of Neeson's brothers said, "I saw the state of my brother's body after he was butchered on the street. I said, 'That is not my brother.' Even our mother would not have recognized him."

On Friday, October 22, UDR soldier Thomas Cochrane was kidnapped by the IRA. Murphy took it upon himself to kidnap a Catholic as hostage in order to secure Cochrane's release. He hijacked a black cab and drove to the Falls Road. Joseph Donegan, a Catholic doing nothing more than making his way home, hailed the cab and got in. Murphy attacked the man immediately as the taxi was driven back to the Shankill area. At a house owned by Murphy in Brookmount Street, Donegan was sadistically tortured by Murphy, who pulled out all but three of his teeth with pliers. Murphy's associate, Tommy Stewart, battered Donegan to death with a shovel. Cochrane's body was found a week later. Murphy's murder by the IRA took place in a loyalist stronghold, and the fact that the IRA knew when and where to find him suggests that the IRA received intelligence from other UVF members who considered Murphy 'out of control'. Murphy's family denied he was a violent man or that he was involved with the Butchers: "My Lenny could not have killed a fly," said his mother Joyce. At the other extreme, William Moore's mother thanked Jimmy Nesbitt, the lead detective in the Butchers investigations, for putting her son behind bars.

UVF insurgency and murders continued into the late 1980s and early 1990s, notably in east Tyrone and north Armagh. The worst atrocity took place on March 3, 1991 with the Cappagh killings when the UVF killed three IRA members and a civilian. The IRA retaliated by executing a number of UVF leaders.

The year before the loyalist ceasefire witnessed some of the worst sectarian murders perpetrated by loyalists during The Troubles. On June 18, 1994, UVF members machine-gunned O'Toole's pub (also known as The Heights Bar) in the Loughinisland massacre in County Down. Reason: the twenty-four customers were watching the Republic of Ireland football team playing Italy in the World Cup on television and were therefore presumed to be Catholics. At 10.10 p.m. two UVF members dressed in boiler suits and balaclavas walked into the bar. One shouted, "Fenian bastards!" and opened fire with a Vz. 58 assault rifle, unleashing into the little room more than sixty bullets. Six people died and five were injured. Barney Green was one of the dead: he was eighty-seven years old. Pope John Paul II, Queen Elizabeth II and US president Bill Clinton all sent messages of sympathy.

Apparently, it was all in retaliation for the June 16, INLA assassination of three UVF members in a drive-by shooting on the Shankill Road. The slaughter followed the UVF shooting dead of a Catholic taxi driver in Carrickfergus and the murder of two Protestant civilians in Newtownabbey, whom they thought were Catholics.

The Loughinisland massacre brought with it more allegations of collusion and cover-up, that police (RUC) double agents or informers in the UVF were linked to the massacre and that police shielded them by destroying evidence and conducting a less than thorough investigation. The fallout was dramatic: in 2011 the Police Ombudsman concluded that there were significant failings in the police investigation, but no evidence that police colluded with the UVF. However, the Ombudsman failed to investigate the role of informers: the report was branded a whitewash and even the Ombudsman's own investigators demanded to be disassociated from it. The report was quashed, the Ombudsman replaced and a new inquiry ordered. The new Ombudsman report in 2016 concluded that there had been collusion between the police and the UVF, and that the investigation was undermined so as to protect informers, but found no evidence police had foreknowledge of the attack. A documentary about the massacre, *No Stone Unturned*, released in November 2017, named the chief suspects, one of whom was a British soldier, and claimed that one of the killers was an informer.

The UVF signed a ceasefire in October 1994 but ceasefire was not welcomed by all. The more militant and radical members of the UVF broke away to form the Loyalist Volunteer Force (LVF), led by Billy Wright. The violence continued, fanned by the January 2000 execution of UVF Mid-Ulster brigadier Richard Jameson by an LVF gunman. At the same time the UVF was also at war with the UDA, a conflict which only ended following seven deaths. Veteran anti-UVF campaigner Raymond McCord estimates that the UVFs killed more than thirty people since its 1994 ceasefire, most of them Protestants. It all erupted again in 2005 when the UVF killed four men in Belfast.

According to CAIN, the UVF killed seventeen active and four former republican paramilitaries. Republicans killed thirteen UVF members, some of whom may well have been exposed as targets for assassination by UVF colleagues. The UVF has the unenviable record of killing more people than any other loyalist paramilitary group. Sutton records that the UVF and The Red Hand Commando (RHC) were responsible for at least 485 killings, and lists a further 256 loyalist killings that have not yet been attributed to one particular group. According to *Lost Lives* (2006), the UVF was responsible for 569 killings: 414 (85%) were civilians, 11 of whom were civilian political activists; 21 (4%) were members or former members of republican paramilitary groups; 44 (9%) were members or former members of loyalist paramilitary groups and 6 (1%) were members of the British security forces. Sixty-six UVF/RHC members and four former members were killed in the conflict

On January 29, 2018 a UVF 'supergrass' who admitted the murders of five people among hundreds of offences had his thirty-five-year jail term reduced to six and a half years for helping the police as a paid informer for eleven years. Gary Haggarty (45) was a former leader of a UVF unit in north Belfast. His crimes were committed during a "terrorist campaign over a 16-year period" between 1991 and 2007. A judge said the offences were "ones of exceptional gravity" but that he had provided significant information. "Exceptional gravity" included beating a man to death with a hammer. After turning state witness in 2009, Haggarty provided information on fifty-five loyalist murders and twenty attempted murders in the course of 1,015 police interviews. However, only one man is to be prosecuted, for two murders, on the back of the evidence. The BBC reported in January 2018: "Haggarty admitted murdering: Catholic Sean McParland, who was shot while babysitting in Belfast in 1994; John Harbinson, a Protestant, who was handcuffed and beaten to death by a UVF gang on the Mount Vernon estate in north Belfast in May 1997;

Catholic workmen Eamon Fox, 44, a father of six, and Gary Convie, 24, a father of one, shot dead as they had lunch together in a car in Belfast's North Queen Street in May 1994; Sean McDermott, a 37-year-old Catholic found shot dead in his car near Antrim in August 1994; He also admitted five attempted murders, including against police officers, 23 counts of conspiracy to murder and directing terrorism. The judge also took into consideration a further 301 lesser offences in his judgement."

Red Hand Commando

Small, discreet, exclusive and highly selective, the Red Hand Commando enjoyed close connections and a shared mission with the UVF. They killed thirteen people during The Troubles: twelve civilians and one of its own. Their secretive and clandestine nature has ensured that they are the only loyalist paramilitary group not to have suffered from a supergrass, or informant. The RHC was formed in 1972, in the Shankill area of west Belfast; they had agreed a union with the UVF whereby in 'operational' matters it shared weapons and personnel and carried out attacks under the UVF banner. Membership exceeded a thousand. A snapshot of their trail of mayhem follows:

February 8, 1972: A member of the Catholic Ex-Servicemen's Association was killed in a drive-by shooting on Crumlin Road, Belfast. July 1974: 'No warning bomb spree' in which the RHC bombed fourteen Catholic-owned pubs in a fortnight. One man was killed and a hundred people were injured. April 12, 1975: The RHC claimed responsibility for a gun and bomb attack on Strand Bar, Anderson Street, Belfast, killing six Catholic civilians. December 19, 1975: An RHC car bomb exploded without warning at Kay's Tavern in Dundalk, County Louth, killing two civilians and wounding twenty. This was followed by a gun and bomb attack on Silverbridge Inn near Crossmaglen, County Armagh. Two Catholic civilians and an English civilian died, six others were wounded. (Members of the Glenanne gang were involved in both attacks.) October 28, 1976: The RHC and Ulster Freedom Fighters claimed responsibility for killing former Sinn Féin vice-president Máire Drumm. She was murdered by gunmen dressed as doctors in Belfast's Mater Hospital. She had just retired and was in hospital for an operation. A UVF member (a former soldier) who worked as a security officer at the hospital was among a number of men jailed for the murder. August 10, 1991: The Loyalist Retaliation and Defence Group (linked to the RHC) shot dead a Catholic civilian at his shop on Donegall Road, Belfast. He was the first of two murdered for selling the republican newsletter *An Phoblacht*. January 1, 1993: Two Catholic civilians on Manor Street, Belfast, were murdered. The two men were cleaning a car when they were shot at from a passing vehicle. The RHC claimed it was revenge for the killing of a British soldier two days before. April 7, 1994: A Protestant woman was found dead at the back of a derelict house on Donegall Avenue, Belfast. She had been beaten and then shot by a group of RHC members who had assumed she was a Catholic. September 28, 1995: The RHC shot dead one of its own members in Bangor, County Down, in an internal dispute. March 17, 1999: The UVF shot dead an expelled member of the RHC as he walked over waste ground off Malvern Way, Belfast, in an internal dispute.

Glenanne Gang

A motley gang of loyalist murderers operating largely in the so-called 'murder triangle' that was counties Armagh and Tyrone. Murder Inc. could just as well describe the forty operators from the three organizations who made up the gang: British soldiers from the Ulster Defence Regiment (UDR), police officers from the Royal Ulster Constabulary (RUC) and members of the Mid-Ulster Brigade of the Ulster Volunteer Force (UVF). 'Glenanne' comes from the farm at Glenanne, near Markethill, County Armagh, used as the gang's arms dump and bomb-making site. For such a small band of insurgents, the death toll racked up in their murder spree was prodigious: various incarnations of the gang are said to be responsible for killing about 120 people—almost all Catholic civilians with no proven links to Irish republican paramilitaries. The Cassel Report looked into seventy-six killings attributed to the group and found evidence that British soldiers and RUC officers were involved in all but two of those. The report also found that some senior RUC and UDR officers knew of the crimes but did nothing "to prevent, investigate or punish". Allegedly, key members acted as double agents working for British military intelligence and RUC Special Branch. Following is a smattering of their killings:

October 4, 1972: Catholic civilian Patrick Connolly was killed and his mother and brother were injured when a grenade was thrown through the window of their house in Portadown. The family were Catholics living in a mixed area of the town. According to the Cassell Report, "the grenade was of a type manufactured in the United Kingdom for use by the British Armed Forces". January 17, 1974: Gun attack on Boyle's Bar in Cappagh, County Tyrone. Two gunmen entered the pub and opened fire indiscriminately. Catholic civilian Daniel Hughes was killed and three others wounded. May 7, 1974: Catholic civilians James and Gertrude Devlin were shot dead near Dungannon, County Tyrone. They were driving home with their seventeen-year-old daughter. As they neared their house, a man in a military uniform stopped the car and opened fire. James and Gertrude were killed outright and their daughter, Patricia, in the back seat, was wounded. UDR soldier William

Thomas Leonard was convicted of the killings. His membership in the UDR was withheld from the courts by the police. April 1, 1975: Killing of Catholic civilian Dorothy Trainor. She and her husband were shot by at least two gunmen as they walked through a park near Garvaghy Road, Portadown. Two of her sons were later killed by loyalists. April 3, 1975: Killing of Catholic civilian Martin McVeigh. He was shot dead near his home at Ballyoran Park, off the Garvaghy Road in Portadown, as he cycled home from work. Robin Jackson, a known gang member, was later arrested in possession of the murder weapon, but the RUC did not question or charge him with the murder. April 21, 1975: Killing of Catholic civilians Marion Bowen who was eight months pregnant, and her brothers, Seamus and Michael McKenna, by a booby-trap bomb left in Bowen's house at Killyliss, near Granville, County Tyrone.

April 27, 1975: Three Catholic civilians were shot at a social club in Bleary, near Ballydougan. August 1, 1975: Gunmen shot up a minibus outside Gilford, near Ballydougan, killing two Catholic civilians and wounding several more. August 24, 1975: Two Catholic civilians were shot dead after being forced from their car at another bogus military checkpoint in Altnamachin. December 19, 1975: Two Catholic civilians were killed and twenty injured when loyalists detonated a car bomb outside a pub in Dundalk. Soon after, they killed three more Catholic civilians and wounded six in a gun and bomb attack on a pub in Silverbridge, near Whitecross. These attacks were coordinated; the Silverbridge attack involved the Glenanne gang. An RUC officer later admitted involvement; detectives believed other RUC officers and a British soldier were also involved.

We have noted how the gang was also implicated in the Dublin and Monaghan slaughters in 1974 and in the Miami Showband murders in 1975. Other atrocities include the Reavey and O'Dowd killings (1976) and, in the same year, the Hillcrest Bar bombing.

New Year 1976 started with tragedy for the Reavey and O'Dowd families when two coordinated gun attacks on January 4, 1976 in County Armagh claimed six Catholics lives: members of the Glenanne Gang burst into their homes and shot them. Three members of the Reavey family were killed at their unlocked (because everyone was welcome there) home in Whitecross; four members of the O'Dowd family were murdered at their home in Ballydougan. Brothers John (24), Brian (22) and Anthony (17) Reavey were watching *Celebrity Squares* on television in the sitting room: the gunmen strafed them with two 9mm Sterling submachine guns, a 9mm Luger pistol and a .455 Webley revolver. John and Brian were killed but Anthony managed to run to the bedroom and take cover under a bed. He was shot several times and left for dead. He crawled about 200 yards to a neighbour's house but died of a brain haemorrhage on January 30. Although the pathologist reported that the shooting played no part in his death, Anthony is listed as a victim of The Troubles.

Eugene Reavey spoke to the *Belfast Telegraph* on January 2, 2016: "My brother found the lads dead. He didn't speak for a year afterwards ... My mother missed those boys every minute of every day until she died three years ago. She would run after young fellows with red hair on the street, thinking they could be Anthony. She'd look in the shops for a jumper that would suit John or a shirt for Brian. She still set the table at night for them. Three extra places—we could never talk her out of it."

Fifteen miles away in Ballydougan at about 6.20 p.m., three masked men burst into the home of the Catholic O'Dowds. Sixteen people filled the house for a family reunion. The men were in the sitting room with some of the children, playing the piano. The gunmen sprayed the room with bullets, killing Joseph O'Dowd (61) and his nephews Barry (24) and Declan O'Dowd (19). While investigating the RUC officers were hostile, unhelpfully asserting, "Your brothers were not shot for nothing." The police inquest, however, found that the families had no links with paramilitaries.

The following day, gunmen pulled up a minibus carrying ten Protestant workmen near Whitecross and shot them dead by the roadside: the Kingsmill massacre. The South Armagh Republican Action Force—a cover for the Provisional IRA South Armagh Brigade—claimed responsibility, saying it was retaliation for the Reavey and O'Dowd killings. The significance of this is that following the massacre, the British government declared County Armagh a Special Emergency Area and announced that the SAS was being posted to South Armagh.

Members of the grieving Reavey family came upon the Kingsmill massacre while driving to hospital to collect the bodies of John and Brian. Some members of the security forces then harassed them and accused Eugene Reavey of organizing the Kingsmill massacre. On their way home from the morgue, the Reavey family was stopped again at a checkpoint where soldiers of the 3rd Battalion, Parachute Regiment assaulted and humiliated Eugene's mother, poked a gun in Eugene's back and danced on his dead brothers' clothes. In 2007, the Police Service of Northern Ireland apologized for the "appalling harassment suffered by the family in the aftermath at the hands of the security forces". After the killings of the Reavey brothers, their father made his five surviving sons swear not to retaliate or to join any republican paramilitary group. In 1999, Democratic Unionist Party (DUP) leader Ian Paisley proclaimed in the House of Commons that Eugene Reavey "set up the Kingsmill massacre". In 2010, a report by the police Historical Enquiries Team absolved Eugene of any involvement. The Reavey family sought an apology, but Paisley refused to retract the allegation.

The Hillcrest Bar bombing, also known as the Saint Patrick's Day bombing, took place on March 17, 1976 in Dungannon, County Tyrone, when the UVF detonated a car bomb outside the Hillcrest Bar—jointly owned by a Catholic and a Protestant—thronged with Catholics celebrating Saint Patrick's Day. Four Catholic civilians were killed, including two thirteen-year-old boys, Patrick Barnard and Jimmy McCaughey who were standing outside on their way to a disco at a school straight across the road. Almost fifty people were injured, nine seriously. Andrew Small (62) was walking past with his wife and was also killed in the blast.

That evening, UVF members had parked a green Austin Healey 1100 outside the Hillcrest Bar. It had been stolen in Armagh nine days earlier. 8.20 p.m. came and the time bomb in the car exploded. The Pat Finucane Centre (PFC) has attributed the bombing to the Glenanne gang. Eddie Barnard, Patrick's elder brother, told the *The Irish Times* of May 2, 2015: "My mother was devastated. She became reliant on Valium, and she used to just sit in tears. But she weaned herself off them. In later life she learned to read and write, which she had never been able to do. She never talked about it, but she took Patrick's school jumper to bed with her every night. It was under her pillow when she died."

Loyalist Volunteer Force

The 300-at most-member-strong LVF can lay claim to at least fourteen murders, mostly of Catholic civilians in random gun and bomb attacks, mostly between 1996 and 1998. The Force was founded by Billy Wright, "the notoriously violent and publicity-minded leader of the mid-Ulster UVF', when he and his unit seceded from the UVF in protest against the ceasefire called by the Combined Loyalist Military Command (CLMC) in October 1994. The LVF ended its campaign in August 1998 and decommissioned some of its weapons; however, a loyalist feud led to more killings in the early 2000s. According to CAIN, the LVF killed eighteen people, which included 13 civilians (11 Catholics and 2 Protestants), 3 UVF members, 1 former Provisional IRA member and 1 of its own (LVF) members. Some of these atrocities took place when on:

July 15, 1997: The LVF killed Catholic Bernadette Martin (18) in Aghalee. She was shot four times in the head as she slept in her Protestant boyfriend's house. July 24, 1997: The LVF kidnapped Catholic civilian James Morgan (16) in Newcastle, County Down. He was tortured, beaten to death with a hammer and his body was then doused in petrol and set alight. His charred and mutilated body was found three days later in a waterlogged ditch used for the disposal of animal carcasses near Clough. December 27, 1997: The LVF attacked the dance hall of the Catholic-owned Glengannon Hotel near Dungannon. Hundreds of teenagers were attending a Christmas disco when gunmen fired on a crowd of people at the entrance. A doorman, Catholic Seamus Dillon (45), was killed and three other people were wounded. This was believed to be revenge for the killing of Billy Wright earlier that day.

Red Hand Defenders

The Red Hand Defenders first came to prominence in 1998, made up of disaffected members of other loyalist paramilitary groups opposed to the Good Friday Agreement: the Loyalist Volunteer Force (LVF), and the UDA/UFF. The RHD's first murder was a bomb attack on September 7, 1998 which killed Frankie O'Reilly, an RUC officer, during an Orange Order demonstration at Drumcree. Since then, the RHD has claimed responsibility for murdering a further ten people, nine civilians and one a former UDA member. The group claimed responsibility for the killings of Brian Service (35), a Catholic civilian, on November 2, and of Rosemary Nelson (40), a leading Catholic human rights solicitor, in Lurgan on March 15, 1999. A bomb exploded under her car. Previously Nelson claimed she and her three children had received death threats from members of the RUC as a result of her work. On May 23, 2011 the inquiry into her assassination found no evidence that state agencies— RUC, British Army and MI5—had "directly facilitated" her murder but "could not exclude the possibility" that individual members had helped the perpetrators. It found that the state had failed to protect her and that some RUC intelligence had "leaked". Both of these factors helped "legitimize her as a target in the eyes of loyalist terrorists". The report also found that RUC officers had publicly abused and assaulted her in 1997, and made threatening remarks about her to her clients, which entered the public domain. Between 1998 and 2003 the RHD was responsible for fifty or so terrorist attacks, many of them involving pipe bombs. In 2001 speculation was rife that the RHD was being used as flag of convenience by members of the LVF and the UDA/UFF to carry out attacks: paramilitary organizations qualified on ceasefire for the early-release scheme for paramilitary prisoners. On September 6, 2013 the RHD allegedly threatened to carry out attacks on children and staff at three Catholic schools in north Belfast.

PART 3: BRITISH SECURITY FORCES

RUC & Special Branch

Between 1922 and 2001 the Royal Ulster Constabulary was Northern Ireland's police force. Founded on June 1, 1922 to succeed the Royal Irish Constabulary (RIC), it had at its peak around 8,500 officers with a further 4,500 members in the RUC Reserve. During The Troubles, 301 RUC officers and eighteen former or retired RUC officers were killed, and almost 9,000 injured in paramilitary assassinations or attacks, mostly by the Provisional IRA; the RUC was the most dangerous police force in the world in which to serve. For their part, the RUC killed fifty-five people, twenty-eight of whom were civilians. The Provisional IRA Newry mortar attack on the RUC station in 1985, which killed nine officers (including two Catholics), was the highest number of deaths inflicted on the RUC in a single incident.

The RUC had a number of systemic problems, the most significant of which was that, as an organization it had always been composed mainly from members of the Protestant community. In 1992, only 7.78% of the full-time force were Catholic, and an even smaller percentage in the reserve forces. The RUC, then, was never representative of the province which it policed.

Given this, it is hardly surprising that the RUC has been accused, and not just by republicans and Irish nationalists, of impartial policing and discrimination, as well as collusion with loyalist paramilitaries and British intelligence units. These allegations prompted several inquiries, one of which, 'Operation Ballast: an investigation into the circumstances surrounding the murder of Raymond McCord Jr' in 1997, was published by Police Ombudsman Nuala O'Loan. The report identified police, CID and Special Branch collusion with loyalist terrorists under thirty separate headings; but no member of the RUC has ever been charged or convicted of any criminal acts as a result of these inquiries. O'Loan concluded that there was no reason to believe the findings of the investigation were isolated incidents. "The investigation has proved the most complex ever undertaken by the Police Ombudsman ... [which] has identified that intelligence held within the policing system, the majority of which has been graded by police as 'reliable and probably true' and which has been corroborated from other sources, which links police informants to: the murders of ten people; 72 instances of other crime, including: ten attempted murders; ten 'punishment' shootings; 13 punishment attacks; a bomb attack in Monaghan; 17 instances of drug dealing, and; additional criminality, including criminal damage, extortion and intimidation ... During this period the Police Ombudsman has estimated that payments of at least £79,840 were made to Informant 1, which included a series of incentive payments ... The Police Ombudsman's Office has encountered a number of difficulties during this investigation, including the fact that a number of documents were either missing, lost or destroyed ... This general absence of records has prevented senior officers from being held to account. The Police Ombudsman is of the view that this was not an oversight but was a deliberate strategy and had the effect of avoiding proper accountability."

Back in 1969 it was the inability of the RUC to deal with The Troubles—notably in the guise of the Ulster Special Constabulary (USC), or the B Specials, who were viewed by some nationalists as more anti-Catholic and anti-nationalist than the RUC—that led to the deployment of the British Army to support the civil administration under Operation Banner. On October 3, 1969 the RUC was radically reorganized and all military duties were transferred to the newly formed Ulster Defence Regiment, which was under military command and replaced the B Specials.

On April 19, 1969 clashes occurred between Northern Ireland Civil Rights Association (NICRA) marchers, the RUC and loyalists in the Derry Bogside. RUC officers entered the house of Samuel Devenny (42), an innocent Catholic, and savagely beat him, two of his teenage daughters and a family friend. One of the daughters was beaten unconscious as she lay recovering from earlier surgery. Devenny suffered a heart attack and died on July 17 from his injuries. On July 13, RUC officers beat up a Catholic civilian, Francis McCloskey (67), during clashes in Dungiven. He died of his injuries the next day.

On August 12, the loyalist Apprentice Boys of Derry were ill-advisedly allowed to march along the perimeter of the Bogside. The nationalists bombarded the RUC with stones and petrol bombs; the RUC, backed by loyalists, in response stormed the Bogside using CS gas, armoured vehicles and water cannons, but were kept at bay by hundreds of nationalists. This, the Battle of the Bogside, lasted for two days. The rioting continued throughout Northern Ireland with the RUC deploying Shorland armoured cars armed with Browning machine guns. The Shorlands twice opened fire on a block of flats in a nationalist district, killing a nine-year-old boy, Patrick Rooney. RUC officers fired on rioters in Armagh, Dungannon and Coalisland.

As we have seen, the first IRA murder inflicted on the RUC came after the Hunt Committee, set up following the Derry riots, published its report on October 12, recommending that the RUC become an unarmed force and the B Specials be stood down. The loyalists reacted badly and, during violence in the

Shankill, UVF members shot dead RUC officer Victor Arbuckle. In August 1970 two constables, Donaldson and Millar, were murdered in a bomb attack in South Armagh. However, it was the RUC Special Branch officer who was target number one: the IRA pledged that they would be "ruthlessly struck down where and whenever they were found". Between 1971 and 1990 ten serving officers were killed—seven Protestants and three Catholics—in nine separate incidents that also caused the deaths of three civilians. Five of these incidents involved off-duty officers.

In late 1982, a number of IRA and INLA volunteers were shot dead by the RUC, leading to accusations that the RUC was pursuing a shoot-to-kill policy. In September 1983, four officers were charged with murder in connection with the deaths but all were subsequently acquited.

On February 28, 1985, the IRA launched a heavy mortar attack on the RUC base at Corry Square in Newry, killing nine RUC officers and injuring almost forty more, the highest death toll ever suffered by the RUC. Nine shells were launched from the back of a lorry parked on Monaghan Street, about 250 yards from the base. At least one 50lb shell landed on a portacabin containing a canteen, where many officers were having their evening tea break.

Collusion was endemic and long-standing. The Special Patrol Group was formed in the late 1960s when it was known as the Police Reserve Force. The unit was a tactical reserve of 150 officers whose role was "to provide backup in civil commotion, to police sensitive areas at times of confrontation, and to show the flag in a disciplined and impressive way to those who wished to break the peace". They were the first policemen trained by the British Army in the use of riot equipment and tactics. As well as their Walther PP pistols (later replaced with .357 magnum Ruger Speed Six revolvers) and batons, each constable sported either a Sterling submachine gun, a Ruger 14 carbine or a 7.62mm SLR rifle. A few officers were issued with Lee-Enfield sniper rifles with telescopic sights. The six-man teams were trained in special weapons and tactics (SWAT) techniques. The unit was rebadged Divisional Mobile Support Unit (DMSU) in 1980 following the conviction of two of its members for kidnap and murder. The two, John Weir and Billy McCaughey, implicated some of their colleagues in crimes including supplying weapons, passing information and providing transport to loyalist paramilitaries as well as carrying out shooting and bombing attacks. Weir alleged that senior officers, including Chief Superintendent Harry Breen, were aware of and rubber-stamped their nefarious activity.

E4A was an intelligence-gathering unit within E Department of the RUC, set up around 1978. Its main role was to carry out surveillance, the fruits of which could

An undercover RUC officer and badge.

be acted on by RUC Special Branch (E4C). E4A was supported by the Headquarters Mobile Support Unit (HMSU). HMSU was a uniformed elite unit which aspired to be the RUC equivalent of the SAS. Members were trained by the SAS on how to confront the IRA and other enemies with "firepower, speed and aggression". The unit had its origins in the elite Bessbrook Support Unit set up in 1977 to take over from the SAS their deployment along the South Armagh border. In 1979 the Bessbrook Support Unit was replaced by the Special Patrol Group which in turn was replaced in 1981 by the Special Support Unit (SSU), subsequently renamed the Headquarters Mobile Support Unit (HMSU).

The SSU was implicated in the alleged shoot-to-kill deaths in November and December 1982 when six republican paramilitaries were shot dead in three separate incidents; all of the insurgents were unarmed. These incidents, and evidence of systematic falsification of the details of the encounters, led to the 1984–86 Stalker Inquiry. Officers selected for the SSU underwent an immensely tough two-week assessment of fitness, mental ability and endurance under pressure, followed by a four-week course including seven days devoted exclusively to weapons training, crucially with the focus being to "eliminate the threat" posed to officers. The training was delivered by the SAS, equivalent to the intense training undergone by Det and MI5.

Collusion apart, from a neutral's point of view, the statistics show that the Special Branch undoubtedly did much that was good and brave. Of the fifty-eight Catholic insurgents killed in forty separate covert operations between 1974 and 1992, 83% were found to have weapons or explosives with them and only one was not confirmed to be an active member of a terrorist organization. Of the seventy-three deaths in total, fifty-eight were Catholic insurgents, six were civilians (two Catholics and four Protestant), eight were security forces personnel and one was a loyalist terrorist. During the time they were being accused of operating a shoot-to kill policy, Special Branch's covert operations, even when the SAS was involved, had an arrest rate of 96%. The remaining 4%, of course, remains significant—shoot to kill is shoot to kill. Eighty-eight percent of the insurgents who died, died in the border counties; eight 'on the runs' were killed from 1983; before that none was. Killings in RUC covert operations between 1974 and 1998 amount to 2% of the total loss of life throughout The Troubles.

Most powerfully, though, it has been estimated that Special Branch saved in the region of 16,500 lives by disrupting 85% of the IRA's operations; so, if these figures are anything near accurate, that is a job well done by any measure.

Fatalities involving E4 SSU include November 11, 1982 in Lurgan when three unarmed IRA men were shot dead. Three E4 officers were later acquitted of murder; November 24, 1982 in Lurgan when Michael Tighe (17), a suspected terrorist; was shot dead. His colleague was arrested and convicted of terrorist offences; December 12, 1982 in Armagh City when two INLA insurgents, unarmed, were shot dead. An E4 officer was later acquitted of murder; November 9, 1989 in north Belfast when an E4 officer died in a friendly-fire incident in a house entry looking for arms.

British Regular Army

In 1969 the British Army was deployed on the streets of Northern Ireland. Their arrival was at first welcomed by the Catholic community, but the bonhomie was short-lived. The number of British soldiers stationed in Northern Ireland fluctuated in response to the security situation. The figures peaked in 1972 at over 30,000. By 1994, it was 18,500. Subsequent to the IRA ceasefire of 1994, this figure was reduced to 17,000. As of the end of 2001 this figure had fallen further to around 13,000.

Killings by the British Army were not confined to cloak and dagger-, intelligence- and surveillance-based activities. Sometimes they were caused by overt indiscipline, gung-ho aggression and shabby leadership.

George Garrigues took this photo from his room in the Europa Hotel during a visit to Belfast. It shows British troops and police, with two vehicles, investigating a couple on the street behind the Europa Hotel, September 1974. The hotel was damaged thirty-three times by explosions, gaining the dubious distinction of being "the most bombed hotel in the world".

The writing's on the wall. 'The Long Walk'—a British Army technical officer approaches a suspect device at the junction of Manor Street and Oldpark Road in Belfast. The ominous quotation on the sign on the building to the left is from the Old Testament, Amos 4:12.

Using a 'wheelbarrow' on the streets of Northern Ireland in 1978. The wheelbarrow was a remotely controlled robot designed in 1972 for use by British Army bomb disposal teams in Northern Ireland (321 EOD), mainland Britain (11 EOD Regiment) and later Iraq. Over 400 have been destroyed in operations but they have saved hundreds of lives.

The carnage after a 1974 bombing.

Two men, Séamas Cusack and Desmond Beattie, were shot dead in separate incidents in the early morning and afternoon of July 8, 1971. They were the first to be killed by the British Army in Derry. In both cases the British Army insisted that the men were attacking them with guns or bombs; eyewitnesses insisted that both were unarmed. The result was a surge of support for the IRA. The British Army post at Bligh's Lane came under sustained attack, and troops there and around the city came under fire from the IRA.

Disarming bombs concealed in drums.

An anti-internment protest organized by the Northern Ireland Civil Rights Association (NICRA) at Magilligan Camp in January 1972 was met with aggression and violence from the 1st Battalion, The Parachute Regiment. NICRA had organized a march from the Creggan to Derry city centre, in defiance of a ban, on the following Sunday, January 30, 1972. Both IRAs were asked, and agreed, to suspend operations on that day to ensure the march passed off peacefully. The British Army erected barricades around the Free Derry area to prevent marchers from reaching the city centre. On the day, march organizers turned the march away from the barriers and up to Free Derry Corner, but some youths proceeded to the barrier at William Street and stoned soldiers. Troops from 1 Para then moved into Free Derry and opened fire, killing thirteen people, all of whom were subsequently found to be unarmed. A fourteenth victim died four months later in June 1972. Like the killing of Cusack and Beattie the previous year, 'Bloody Sunday' had the effect of hugely increasing recruitment to the IRA, even among previous moderates.

Father Edward Daly, later Bishop Daly, waves a blood-stained handkerchief in his brave attempt to rescue a wounded civilian shot by the Parachute Regiment.

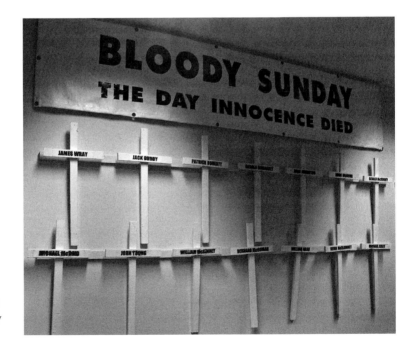

Banner and crosses worn by the families of the 'Bloody Sunday' victims on the annual commemoration march. (Photo by Sean Mack)

Special Air Service

The SAS emerged on the scene in 1973, but in a training and advisory role tasked with setting up the highly professional and successful 14 Intelligence Company, 'The Det'.

The IRA had blown the cover of the SAS's predecessors, the Mobile Reconnaissance Force (MRF), and now the SAS was laying the foundations for 14 Intelligence, a unit that would act as their eyes and ears providing high-grade surveillance and intelligence support, and some firepower when required. A special training wing of the SAS recruited and trained recruits while SAS officers formed most of the command staff.

It was not until 1976, with the crises in Northern Ireland deteriorating by the day, that the prime minister, Harold Wilson, publicly announced that units of 22 Special Air Service were to be posted to Ulster. Many saw this as part of the answer to an increasingly intractable problem while others saw it as exactly the kind of thing that was not needed. Tact, negotiation and diplomacy were what was required and these were not qualities for which the SAS was noted. Nothwithstanding, A, B, D and G squadrons were slated to rotate in and out of Northern Ireland on a four-to-six-month month schedule. The following, by no means comprehensive, gives an idea of the sort of activities the SAS were engaged in.

Things got off to a bad start in January when a twelve-man troop from D squadron was deployed to Bessbrook, the scene of a recent terrorist attack on a bus. This deployment was publicized, placing the usually clandestine SAS squarely in the spotlight—nothing short of anathema to the regiment. This initial deployment was soon bolstered by the rest of D squadron to carry out surveillance and intelligence-gathering, by way of foot patrols and covert observation positions (OPs).

In March 1976 suspected IRA commander Sean McKenna was abducted from his home in the Republic by the SAS and dumped over the border where he was promptly arrested by a regular army unit. In April 1976 an SAS team manning OPs overlooking his house arrested another suspected IRA man, Peter Cleary (25). Cleary was killed by the SAS while allegedly trying to escape. He was unarmed. In May 1976 an SAS team in an unmarked car 'strayed' across the border with the Republic and was arrested by Irish police. The first car was followed by two more SAS cars full of armed troopers that were also arrested in a controversial and politically embarrassing incident. April 1977 saw the SAS ambush and kill IRA man, Seamus Harvey, acting on a tip-off; they engaged but failed to capture several of his accomplices.

In February 1978 the SAS ambushed a two-man IRA team as they attempted to access a weapons cache on a County Tyrone farm. Paul Duffy (23) was killed. The other terrorist was wounded but managed to drive away. June 1978 saw a four-man IRA team attempt to firebomb Ballysillan post office depot. A joint SAS/

RUC team had been tipped-off about the IRA operation and as the three IRA men approached the target, they were ambushed and killed. Two innocent bystanders were challenged by the SAS and one, William Hanna (27), was shot dead when he ran away. In July 1978 sixteen-year-old John Boyle discovered an IRA arms cache in a churchyard in Dunloy, County Antrim. The police learned of this and the SAS set up covert OPs to watch the cache. Young Boyle then returned to the cache, presumably unable to curb his curiosity; mistaking him for an IRA volunteer, a two-man SAS OP team opened fire and killed the boy. The tragedy was a propaganda gift for Sinn Féin, the IRA's political wing. The SAS soldiers were tried and acquitted.

In the early 1980s, Special Forces in Northern Ireland were restructured so that smaller troops of around twenty SAS would be deployed for year-long tours, organized, along with 14 Int, under the umbrella command of Intelligence and Security Group (NI) or Int & Sy Group or simply 'The Group'. These longer tours allowed the SAS men to acquire deeper local knowledge. The Special Projects anti-terrorist team at Hereford were put on-call should reinforcements be needed.

May 1980 saw something of a bungle when an IRA team was cornered in a residential area of Belfast; in response, an SAS unit arrived in unmarked cars but stormed the wrong house enabling the IRA to open up on the SAS team with an M-60 machine gun mounted in a bedroom window. SAS Captain Herbert Westmacott (28) was killed and the IRA team surrendered to regular units.

In January 1981 Sinn Fein politician, Bernadette McAliskey and her husband were shot by loyalist gunmen at their home in Coalisland. An SAS OP had the house under surveillance but did not arrest the gunmen until after the shooting. In March 1981, following a meticulous surveillance operation by 14 Int, four IRA men surrendered to the SAS when they were surrounded in a farmhouse. In December 1981 the SAS, tipped off by an informer, ambushed three IRA men as they collected a cache of firearms from a hedgerow near Coalisland. The IRA members arrived by car: one stayed with the car while the other two approached the cache and were challenged by the SAS troops: Col McGirr was killed outright and Brian Campbell fatally wound. The other IRA man fled the scene, successfully crashing through an SAS cut-off unit who opened fire. His shot-up and blood-stained car was later found some distance away. At least one SAS member was subsequently RTU'd (returned to unit) for failing to prevent the escape.

In July 1984 the SAS was tipped off about a planned IRA attack on a kitchen fittings factory in Ardboe, Tyrone. The SAS set up an ambush and opened fire, wounding one man, William Price (28) who was pursued into a field and shot dead. Two other IRA men were arrested at the scene while a fourth escaped. In October 1984 RUC

Special Branch received a tip-off about IRA plans to kill an off-duty UDR soldier near Dungannon as he drove past a road junction that opened into a haulage yard. The SAS set up OPs and cut-off groups around the area. Several SAS lay in wait in unmarked Q cars. On the morning of the October 18, an IRA unit hijacked a van to use in the attack. As the van drove into the ambush area, the SAS attempted to block it but the van got through. The SAS opened fire at the van. Frederick Jackson (43), an innocent civilian who was driving out of the haulage yard, was struck by a single round and later died. An SAS Q car chased the van, its occupants firing through the windscreen with Heckler & Koch 53 assault rifles. An IRA gunman returned fire from the back of the van and escaped.

On the night of December 1, 1984, following a tip-off about a planned IRA 1,000-pound landmine ambush, two SAS Q cars were on the hunt for a Toyota van believed to be involved. Spotting a suspicious-looking van, the two cars formed a roadblock at both ends of the road where the van was parked. However, they had inadvertently stopped right next to where an IRA unit was making ready a roadside bomb, behind a hedge. The IRA men opened fire on the SAS men as they approached the van, killing Lance-Corporal Alistair Slater before fleeing across fields. The SAS returned fire but two of the gunmen escaped across the border. A third, Kieran Fleming (25), was later found drowned in a river. A fourth IRA man in the Toyota van was shot and killed by the SAS.

In December 1984 the SAS was tipped off about IRA plans to execute a UDR reservist who worked at Gransha hospital in Derry; the SAS, the Det and Special Branch, put the area under surveillance. The undercover soldiers waited in unmarked Q cars for the IRA to make their move. After several nights, on the night of December 6, the soldiers spotted two IRA men on a motorcycle enter the hospital grounds. Seeing a pistol in the passenger's hand, a Q car rammed into the motorbike, causing the passenger to fall off. Three SAS soldiers engaged both the driver and his fallen passenger, leaving Daniel Doherty (23) and William Fleming (19) dead. William was the cousin of Kieran Fleming killed two days earlier.

The SAS set up a three-man OP overlooking a suspected IRA arms cache near Strabane in February 1985. On the night of the 23rd, three IRA men approached to return their assault rifles, petrol bombs and anti-armour grenades to the cache. The SAS engaged them with HK53s, killing all three. In February 1986 the SAS shot dead a man handling a weapon from a cache located in the garden of a house in Toomebridge. Neither the man who was shot nor the two other men who had driven him to the cache were IRA or INLA terrorists: they might have been forced by the IRA into retrieving the weapons for them as they believed that the army had the cache under surveillance.

August 1988 saw three IRA men ambushed and killed by an SAS unit near the town of Drumnakilly, County Tyrone. The IRA Active Service Unit (ASU) was aiming to gun down an off-duty UDR soldier as he repaired his broken-down lorry. The UDR man was, in fact, an SAS trooper and the breakdown was designed to lure the IRA unit into an attack. The IRA unit drove up and one gunman leaned out of the car window, firing an AK-47 at the SAS man who leaped for cover. Eight SAS troopers with G3 rifles in the hedgerows and a GPMG machine-gunner in a derelict farm building all opened fire, unleashing 236 rounds. The IRA team comprising Gerard Harte, Martin Harte and Brian Mullin were all killed.

In March 1988, British intelligence picked up information of an IRA plot to attack a parade of British military bands in Gibraltar; namely, the changing of the guard outside the governor's residence, 'The Convent'. A swift and decisive response was needed. Accordingly, an SAS unit was tasked with intercepting the IRA cell in an operation dubbed Flavius. Spanish security services had been watching a three-person Provisional IRA cell for some weeks, a cell made up of two men and a woman, Danny McCann, Sean Savage and Mairead Farrell, "three of the IRA's most senior activists". Savage was an explosives expert and McCann "a high-ranking intelligence operative"; both McCann and Farrell had previously served prison sentences for offences relating to explosives. The operation was confirmed in November 1987 when several known IRA members were spotted travelling from Belfast to Spain under false identities. MI5 and the Spanish authorities discovered that an IRA active service unit was operating from the Costa del Sol; the members of the unit were then placed under surveillance. Back in Gibraltar a known IRA member was sighted at the changing of the guard ceremony at 'The Convent' which led the British authorities to suspect that the IRA was planning a car-bomb attack when the British soldiers assembled for the ceremony in a nearby carpark. In an attempt to confirm this, the government of Gibraltar suspended the ceremony in December 1987, the pretext being a need to repaint the guardhouse. Their suspicions were confirmed when the same IRA member reappeared at the ceremony when it resumed in February 1988. The SAS underwent training in arrest techniques, while the Gibraltar authorities located a suitable place to hold the would-be bombers after their arrest. The Anglo-Spanish plan was that the SAS would help the Gibraltar police to arrest the IRA members—identified by MI5 officers who had been in Gibraltar for several weeks—if they were seen parking a car in Gibraltar and then attempting to leave the territory.

The IRA plan seems to have been to cross over into Gibraltar, place explosives in the boot of a car at the carpark assembly point and detonate it remotely. Thus on March 6 Savage drove into Gibraltar in a white Renault 5 at 12.45 p.m. An MI5 officer recognized him and he was followed, but he was not positively identified for almost ninety minutes. Things started to move rapidly: Savage was observed parking the white Renault in the carpark, arousing suspicions that it might be full of explosives; reports were then received that McCann and Farrell had crossed the border from Spain into Gibraltar and were heading into town, obviously kept under surveillance, possibly by Det operatives. At around 1450 Savage was seen meeting with McCann and Farrell. Savage then went back into town while the other two headed back to the border. When the coast was clear, one of the SAS team, not an explosives expert, did a walk-by to detect giveaway signs of a car bomb such as exposed antennas, wires or depressed axles caused by a large weight in the boot. Nothing of particular note was seen, of course, it being a 'clean', decoy car. Nevertheless, it was decided that the Renault probably did contain a bomb. The local police chief signed over control of the operation to the SAS. The SAS troopers wore civilian clothing, were equipped with covert radios and carried 9mm Browning Hi-Power pistols. They split into groups to follow both Savage and McCann and Farrell and prepared to move in.

At the same time as the police handed control over to the SAS, they began making arrangements for the IRA operatives once they were in custody, including finding a police vehicle in which to transport the prisoners. A patrol car containing Inspector Luis Revagliatte and three other uniformed officers, apparently on a routine patrol and with no knowledge of Operation Flavius, was ordered to urgently return to police headquarters but was stuck in heavy traffic. Revagliatte's driver activated the siren on the police car in order to hasten the journey back to HQ, thus spooking McCann and Farrell at a Shell petrol station. McCann then reportedly made eye contact with one of the SAS men who later described how he drew his pistol and was on the point of issuing a challenge when "events overtook the warning" as McCann's right arm "moved aggressively across the front of his body", a gesture which could be read as McCann going for his gun or for the car bomb's remote detonator. He shot McCann once in the back. Farrell, meanwhile, was allegedly rummaging in her bag as the SAS operator shot her in the back, before returning to McCann finishing him off with three shots, once in the body and twice in the head. Moments later a second SAS man shot Farrell twice more, then McCann once or twice, before revisiting Farrell and shooting her a further three times. (One of the bullets that passed through Farrell grazed a passerby.)

Down the road Savage was challenged to stop by the other two SAS troopers who had their pistols trained on him. Apparently, Savage ignored this challenge and reached inside his jacket so one of the SAS opened fire. Soldier 'C' shot Savage six times while Soldier 'D' fired nine times.

Police cars converged as the SAS donned berets and armbands to identify themselves. The SAS personnel soon left Gibraltar on an RAF aircraft. Inquiries resulting from keys found on Farrell's body led authorities to a second car, a red Ford Fiesta containing a large quantity of Semtex, 200 rounds of ammunition, four detonators and two timers in a carpark in Marbella. A subsequent inquest found that it was technically possible for the IRA cell to have remotely triggered a car bomb from where the shootings took place.

Despite initial praise for averting mass murder, controversy was not far behind when it was realized that none of the three IRA members had been armed and no remote bomb trigger was to be found. The Renault, of course, contained no explosives. The incident was now seen by some as a summary execution by the army of unarmed paramilitaries in pursuance of a shoot-to-kill policy: another propaganda coup for the IRA. Professor Alan Watson, a British forensic pathologist, carried out the post-mortem examination of the bodies. When he arrived in Gibraltar the day after the shootings the bodies had been taken to the Royal Navy hospital where they had been stripped of their clothing, causing problems in distinguishing entry and exit wounds. The mortuary had no X-ray machine which would have allowed Watson to track the paths of the bullets through the bodies and he was refused access to any other X-ray machine. On returning to Scotland, he was not permitted access to the results of blood tests and other evidence which had been sent for analysis. He was unhappy with the photographs taken by the Gibraltar police photographer. Altogether a puzzling lack of assistance, bordering on the obstructive. Things got murkier. Watson founded that McCann had been shot four times: once in the jaw, once in the head and twice in the back. Farrell was shot five times: twice in the face and three times in the back. Watson estimated that Savage was possibly shot as many as eighteen times. Patrick McGrory, for the families of the victims, asked Watson whether he would agree that Savage's body was "riddled with bullets" and Watson made headlines when he replied: "I concur with your word. Like a frenzied attack." Watson also agreed that the evidence suggested the deceased were shot while on the ground; a second pathologist called by McGrory offered similar findings. Two weeks later, the court heard that David Pryor—a forensic scientist working for the Metropolitan Police— had analyzed the clothes of the deceased and told the inquest his analysis had been hampered by the condition of the clothing when it arrived. Pryor offered evidence contradictory to that given by Soldiers 'A' and 'B' about their proximity to McCann and Farrell when they opened fire: the soldiers claimed they were at least six feet away but Pryor's analysis was that McCann and Farrell were shot from a distance of no more than two or three feet.

After the inquest verdict, the governor of Gibraltar, Air Chief Marshal Sir Peter Terry, declared, "Even in this remote place, there is no place for terrorists." In an act of revenge for his role in Operation Flavius, Terry and his wife, Lady Betty, were shot and seriously injured in front of their daughter when IRA paramilitaries opened fire in their Staffordshire home in September 1990.

Two thousand people met the coffins in Dublin, which were then driven north to Belfast (in 2017 the release of official papers revealed that Taoiseach Charles Haughey had secretly requested that the RAF fly the bodies directly to Belfast). Troops and police saturated the neighbourhoods where McCann, Farrell and Savage had lived to suppress public displays of sympathy. Later that evening, a local IRA member, Kevin McCracken, was shot and allegedly beaten to death by a group of soldiers he had been attempting to shoot. The tension between mourners and police continued until the procession split to allow the hearses to travel to the respective family homes, and then on to Milltown cemetery. Here, the RUC agreed to maintain a low profile at the funeral in exchange for guarantees from the families that there would be no salute by masked gunmen. This agreement was leaked to Michael Stone, a self-styled "freelance Loyalist paramilitary", with fatal consequences, as mentioned earlier.

On September 30, 1988, the inquest jury returned a verdict of "lawful killing". When the families of Savage, McCann and Farrell then took the case to the European Court of Human Rights in 1995 the court found that the British government had violated Article 2 of the European Convention on Human Rights as the authorities' failure to arrest the suspects at the border, combined with the information given to the soldiers, rendered the use of lethal force almost inevitable. It also ruled that the three IRA had been engaged in an act of terrorism, and consequently dismissed unanimously the applicants' claims for damages and costs. Gibraltar was the trigger for a sequence of terrible events in a two-week period: the Milltown Cemetery attack and the Corporals' Killings in Belfast.

The clinical British Army operation at Loughgall in County Armagh marked a significant turning point in The Troubles. It was a huge propaganda success for the British Army, the SAS, the covert intelligence services and the British government; by the same token it dealt a massive blow to the Provisional IRA and to Sinn Féin, and to the East Tyrone brigade in particular. Crucially, it eliminated eight active and dangerous PIRA insurgents in one fell swoop and weakened the East Tyrone brigade irreparably. It was the IRA's biggest reverse in a single operation since the Anglo-Irish War of 1919–22 when twelve paramilitaries were exterminated by the notorious 'Black and Tans'. Indeed, Loughgall clearly demonstrated to the IRA that the British forces were capable of giving as good as they got, and that the fight was now truly on.

When Anthony Hughes (36) and his brother Oliver drove home from work into the usually quiet village of Loughgall in the early evening of May 8, 1987 they could have had no idea what kind of hell they were heading into. The brothers had received a phone call on the morning of the May 8, to repair a lorry belonging to Mr John Guy at Loughgall. They arrived at Guy's house at around 4 p.m. in Anthony's car, a white Citroën GS Special registration number OIA 3248. Having checked the lorry, they had to travel to Donnelly's garage just off the main Armagh–Moy road to get some parts. They then returned to Loughgall to Guy's house to do the repairs. On their return home they decided to travel through Loughgall, as it was a "straighter road".

An eight-man squad of the Provisional IRA East Tyrone brigade chose that night to launch a carefully planned attack on the RUC barracks in the village. A senior IRA figure has said that between thirty and forty people were involved in organizing the attack including members of the attack team, scouts, back-up crews and the peripheral people who provided safe houses and transported paramilitaries and weapons.

Meanwhile, the day before at about 8.30 p.m., twenty-four SAS and Det soldiers and members of the RUC special task force were briefed at Mahon Road Barracks in Portadown about an impending attack on Loughgall RUC barracks. The SAS soldiers had been flown in from their base in Hereford. The Det contingent was already operational in the province. The RUC officers arrived at the barracks between 1 a.m. and 2.30 a.m. on May 8. About an hour later the SAS and Det soldiers arrived at Loughgall and took up their various positions in and around the barracks. Soldiers were armed with GPMGs, Heckler & Koch rifles, pistols, personal radios. Two of the soldiers carried caltrops (spiked anti-vehicular weapons) and were positioned at opposite ends of the Loughgall Road.

All of the IRA attackers came heavily armed, kitted out in bulletproof vests, boiler suits, gloves and balaclavas. The digger, driven by Declan Arthurs (21), was preceded by a scout car carrying two more IRA. The rest of the assault unit travelled in a blue Toyota HiAce van, presumably also with a scout car. They drove past the police station, U-turned and drove back again, twice, presumably to ensure that all was in order. Despite some uneasiness that all was not in order, the unit, after some deliberation, decided to go ahead with the attack. Arthurs, however, had seen the RUC police car in the road when he expected it to be at the station and was concerned that the village was unusually quiet for an early evening. From depositions read at the inquest in June 1995 the van and digger were seen passing the barracks at least three times prior to the attack. One witness stated that it was travelling so slowly that a policeman could have stood out in front of it.

Tony Gormley and Gerard O'Callaghan alighted from the van and joined Arthurs on the digger; at about 7.15 p.m., Declan Arthurs drove the digger towards the base, crashing it through the perimeter fence, its raised bucket carrying 200–400lb of Semtex concealed inside an oil drum, covered with rubble and wired to two forty-second fuses. Arthurs smacked into a blast wall at the entrance of the barracks before jumping clear of the digger. Meanwhile, the rest of the unit arrived on the scene with Eugene Kelly driving; Patrick Kelly was in the passenger seat and in the back were Jim Lynagh, Pádraig McKearney and Seamus Donnelly. They leaped out of the van, lit the fuses and proceeded to strafe the barracks. Simultaneously, the bomb detonated, destroying the digger along with most of the building and injuring three members of the security forces inside.

The paramilitaries had no reason to believe that the building was not manned as usual at that time of day—nothing more than, at most, the usual three RUC officers completing paperwork at the end of their shift. Not so: the British security forces had gathered meticulous, high-grade intelligence about the raid from surveillance by RUC Special Branch (E4A) and the British Army's crack Special Reconnaissance Unit (SRU) with their ubiquitous 'bugs' and human 'eyes-on' observation. Some sources say the security forces were assisted by an RUC informer within the brigade who died at the scene, or through a telephone tap.

Whatever, a sophisticated operation, Operation Judy, was conceived to ambush the attackers. A few hours earlier, two RUC Headquarters Mobile Support Unit (HMSU) officers were posted at the station with the regular local RUC officer who would continue with the normal running of the station and raise no suspicion should the insurgents come knocking on the door. They were reinforced by six SAS soldiers in civilian clothes inside the station, including the operation commander. Outside, a further eighteen soldiers—SAS in uniform and Det in plainclothes—were concealed in woods in five locations around the barracks. The idea was to establish a triangular formation designed to eliminate everybody in the kill zone while reducing the risk of friendly fire.

At the time, the IRA was on a roll: its weapon dumps were filled with over 130 tons of heavy weaponry and high explosives smuggled into Ireland by Colonel Gaddafi of Libya. Its ranks had been reinforced by the IRA's mass breakout from the Maze prison a few years earlier.

The bomb had been ferried across Lough Neagh, from Ardboe to Maghery to avoid security checkpoints. As the crow flies, the route from Ardboe to Loughgall would have taken the bomb team through mainly nationalist districts along the lough shore until they crossed the M1 motorway and into largely unionist districts of north Armagh. The van and digger had been hijacked hours before the attack. At about 2.30 p.m. two armed, hooded men approached Peter Corr at a snooker club on Mountjoy Road, Dungannon. They asked for the keys of a blue Toyota HiAce van registration number GJI 4417 parked outside. Corr was the driver of the van, which belonged to his employer Colm McGrath. Corr was ordered not to report the van missing for four hours. After the men left, Corr phoned McGrath to tell him what had happened. McGrath did not telephone the RUC until 6.50 p.m. At some point during the afternoon three of the soldiers later said that they were made aware of the blue HiAce Van and its registration number and of the possibility that it might be used in the attack on the barracks. At around 6 p.m. three men entered the home of Mrs Josephine Mackle at Aghinlig Upper Dungannon. They told her they were taking her digger, a backhoe loader. The digger was taken from the yard at approximately 6.45 p.m. Two IRA members remained at the farm to prevent the owners from raising the alarm.

The Loughgall plan was nothing new; it was the latest instance of IRA strategy in the area, adapted for the province in the 1980s from a Maoist military theory by Jim Lynagh. This involved creating no-go areas in which the British Army and Royal Ulster Constabulary had no control: South Armagh area was already a liberated zone in which British troops and the RUC did not travel by road because of the threat from roadside bombs and long-range fire. Lynagh was working on the same for his East Tyrone Brigade: his plan was to expel the British security forces from east Tyrone by destroying isolated rural police stations using flying columns and intimidating or killing any building contractors who were employed to rebuild them. From 1985 the brigade enjoyed a successful five-year campaign in which thirty-three security facilities were destroyed and nearly a hundred seriously damaged. The brigade had already carried out spectacular attacks on RUC bases: one was on Ballygawley barracks in County Tyrone, about thirteen miles southwest of Dungannon; another was an assault on The Birches, a small village in northern County Armagh, six miles northwest of Portadown. The MO was familar: the attack began by driving a JCB digger with a 200lb bomb in its bucket through the reinforced fences, exploding the bomb and strafing the police station with gunfire. On both occasions the stations were destroyed; at Ballygawley two RUC officers were shot dead and a further three wounded. The republican magazine *Iris* (No. 11, October 1987) described the attack: "One [IRA] volunteer took up a position close to the front gate. Two RUC men opened the gate and the volunteer calmly stepped forward, shooting them both dead at point blank range. Volunteers firing AK-47 and ArmaLite rifles moved into the barracks, raking it with gunfire. Having secured the building they planted a 100lb bomb inside. The bomb exploded, totally destroying the building after the volunteers had withdrawn to safety."

To emphasize their ruthless intent, in April 1987 a five-man IRA squad shot Harold Henry (52)—a member of the Henry Brothers construction firm that carried out repairs on security force bases—dead. Just before midnight, the IRA took Henry from his home, put him up against a wall and shot him dead with two rifles and a shotgun. He left a widow and six children. To the IRA he was a legitimate target, the first of more than twenty collaborators executed by the IRA for "assisting the British war machine". One of the weapons used in the Henry murder was later retrieved at Loughgall.

The attack on the station at Loughgall was planned to take place after 7 p.m. The actual attack took place at 7.25 p.m. According to locals, the station would have been empty at this time on a Friday evening. Accordingly, it has been claimed that the IRA were solely intent on bombing the barracks rather than killing officers inside. With the best will in the world, the precedent set at The Birches invalidates this: the IRA plan was surely to blow up and destroy the police station, rake it with fire, kill the RUC officers, then escape over the border in the van. Moreover, other evidence suggests strongly that it was not unusual for RUC officers to still be at the station as late as 8 p.m. ploughing through the day's paperwork.

The lethal IRA Active Service Unit (ASU) assembled for Loughall was no ordinary team. It included two veteran, high-level and influential terrorists who were 'on-the-runs' from the law in Northern Ireland and living just over the border. As noted, Patrick McKearney (32) was the architect of the IRA's strategy of attacking security force bases in the south of the province and killing contractors who tried to repair them so as to deny the British 'the ground'. James Lynagh (32) was the other driving force. Patrick Kelly (30) was the leader. Four friends from the village of Cappagh had joined the IRA after the death of one of their friends, Martin Hurson, on hunger strike in 1981. Forensic tests carried out on the IRA weapons retrieved at Loughgall were linked to eight recent murders and thirty-three shootings in the area. To impressionable young volunteers Kelly and McKearney were icons; to the RUC Special Branch they were "streetwise homicidal maniacs" and a serious impediment to peace.

All that Friday, the country lanes around Loughgall were under thorough surveillance and patrolled by Det operators in their unmarked cars looking for signs of the insurgents. One of the Det, a women called 'Anna', tells how she spotted the JCB which at first she and her colleague took for a slow-moving vehicle but when they realized it was a JCB put two and two together and concluded Ballygawley and The Birches: "You suddenly realize it's the MO used by the East Tyrone Brigade. It was like a replay. But this time we were on top of it and we knew what was happening. So we passed on the information to the TCG and pulled off." (The TCG

What was left of the police station.

was the nearby Tasking and Co-Ordinating Group from which the ambush was directed.)

Back at the ambush, the bomb duly exploded and destroyed most of the base; when the IRA opened fire the SAS in the barrack building returned fire; the SAS and Det positioned around the station joined in with M16 and H&K G3 rifles and two L7A2 GPMGs. Six hundred spent cartridge cases from the SAS and Det were recovered from the scene; the van was peppered with approximately 125 bullet holes. Seventy-eight spent cartridges were found fired by IRA weapons. The eight IRA members were killed: all had multiple wounds and all had been shot in the head. Unarmed Declan Arthurs was shot in a lane opposite Loughgall Football Club; a lighter was found which he would have used to light the fuses. Allegedly three wounded IRA members were shot dead as they lay on the ground after surrendering. The IRA members in the scout cars escaped, but only after a tense confrontation with SAS soldiers whom they fully expected to shoot them with their M16 ArmaLites. Apparently, 'regular' soldiers then arrived on the scene via a helicopter which had landed nearby at which point the SAS 'disappeared'. One of the drivers of the escape cars alleges: "We sat there frozen," he said. "There was an auld pair behind us and at this stage there was five or six Brits around. I swore I was going to be dragged out." Then suddenly he, the elderly couple and the other IRA men were ordered by a British soldier to turn their vehicles around and leave the area.

Also killed in the ambush was the RUC agent. It was during the firefight that the Hughes brothers were shot up, caught in the crossfire some 130 yards from the base. To maintain the tightest security the area around the police station had not been cordoned off and no one was evacuated. The British soldiers presumably took the men to be members of the ASU or mistook their white Citroën GS Special

One of the victims, Patrick Kelly, with a G3 rifle on his chest

The shot-up Toyota van. Seamus Donnelly is slumped behind the wheel; the covered bodies of some of his colleagues are just visible on the right.

for an IRA scout car; the fact that Oliver was wearing a boiler suit similar to those worn by the terrorists only added to the confusion. The SAS unleashed their firepower on the vehicle from behind, killing Anthony Hughes, the driver, and seriously wounding his brother Oliver in the head. He later said no warning was given; the car had approximately thirty-four bullet holes in it, twenty-six fired from behind. The RUC chief constable, Sir Ronnie Flanagan, in 2001 described the attack on the two innocent men as "an unspeakable tragedy" and blamed the IRA, not planning or operational shortcomings, for his death. Anthony Hughes's widow was later compensated by the British government for the death of her husband.

Another car, carrying three women, also strayed into the danger zone and came under fire from the insurgents but was successfully shepherded away by SAS soldiers. A man who jumped from his car was protected by the soldiers as was a woman and child in another car.

Recently declassified documents have revealed that ballistic tests on weapons found on the dead were used in some fifty-odd previous murders, including every republican killing in Fermanagh and Tyrone that year (1987). The security forces recovered eight firearms from the scene: three H&K G3 rifles, one FN FAL rifle, two FN FNC rifles, a Franchi SPAS-12T shotgun and a Ruger Security-Six revolver. The Ruger had been plundered from Reserve RUC officer William Clement, killed two years earlier in the attack on Ballygawley RUC base by the same IRA unit. Another of the guns had been used in the killing of Harold Henry, the contractor to the British Army and RUC. In total three civilian contractors had been murdered in the counties that year.

Among republicans the eight insurgents killed in the ambush became known as the 'Loughgall Martyrs'. They were East Tyrone commander Patrick Kelly (32), Declan Arthurs (21), Seamus Donnelly (19), Tony Gormley (25), Eugene Kelly (25) James Lynagh (31), Patrick McKearney (32) and Gerard O'Callaghan (29).

Immediately after the firefight all the SAS and Det soldiers were airlifted out of Loughgall back to Mahon Road station in Portadown. Each soldier was interviewed between 3.25 p.m. on May 9 and 9.35 p.m. on May 12, some four days after the incident. "We can see the immediate aftermath from the Pat Finucane Centre website: "Dr Garvin from County Armagh was called to the scene at 9.45 p.m. May 8. He examined the nine bodies and confirmed them dead. Alistair Black, an RUC sergeant, arrived on the scene at 7.35 p.m. and set up a vehicle checkpoint. He spoke to the soldiers. He preserved the scene until Detective Superintendent Neilly arrived on the scene at 8.22 p.m. Alwyn John Graham, a scenes of crime officer, was requested to attend Mahon Road Station at 10.05 p.m. On arrival he was briefed on his duties. He took possession of the firearms of the soldiers and packaged and labelled them. Constable William John Crompton, a scenes of crime officer, arrived at the scene of the incident at 9.56 p.m. He examined the scene and noted the position of the vehicles and bodies. During the course of his examination Constable Lenaghan, a police photographer, arrived at the scene and took photographs. At 11.15 p.m. Constable Crompton was joined by Dr Murray, Brooks and Wall, all scientists from the N.I. Forensic Laboratory and at 11.17 p.m. by Constable Alexander and Anderson, both members of the Mapping Section. Constable Crompton briefed all on his observations and assisted Mr Wallace with the removal of all nine bodies from the scene and the packaging of IRA weapons. Mr Crompton left the scene at 2.47 a.m. and returned the next morning at 10.34 a.m. to continue his examination of the vehicles and area." Based on the post-mortem reports alone, the authors of the website go on to conclude that the killings were consistent with a shoot-to-kill operation,

All the eight IRA men killed had multiple bullet wounds aimed directly above waist level. According to pathologists reports there were very few injuries to the lower limbs. Almost all of the dead had gunshot wounds to the head. Here is one of the commentaries taken from the autopsy report on Jim Lynagh: "He had been hit by a number of bullets and fragments which had caused holes of varying size and raggedness on the face; the back and left side of the neck; the right shoulder; and both lower limbs. A few of these holes could have been uncomplicated bullet wounds but most were due to bullets which were either deformed or had fragmented after striking the van, whilst others were due to fragments of metal from the bodywork of the van ... There was an entrance hole on the right side of the head just at the top of the ear and some small fragments of bullet were recovered from within it. The underlying skull was fractured and the brain lacerated. Another missile had struck the right side of the face fracturing the cheek bone. It had gone upwards through the base of the skull, lacerating the brain and transecting the brainstem, to probably lodge in the left side of the base of the skull. A bullet had struck the right side of the face over the lower jaw, which was fractured. The bullet had lacerated the pharynx, the back of the tongue and the upper part of the gullet and had fractured the hyoid bone and the voice box. The combined effects of these injuries would have caused rapid death.

The autopsy commentary on Seamus Donnelly strongly suggests that the victim was dispatched at close range: "There was a zone of punctate discharge abrasion surrounding the entrance bullet wound on the front of the neck. This extended onto the face and the front of the left shoulder. Its appearance indicates that when the gun was discharged the muzzle of the weapon was probably within several feet of the body, probably whilst this man was lying on the ground."

An independent pathologist, Dr Hiroshi Nakazawa, has since reported that "Initially, I note that autopsies of nine individuals were performed over a two-day period of time … Conducting these four autopsies in a back-to-back fashion is not a preferred practice and provides little time for the Pathologist to properly evaluate all pathology issues with an autopsy... the autopsy regarding Declan J. Arthurs also demonstrates that evidence of firing at a close range was present. The autopsy report of Gerard M. O'Callaghan likewise demonstrates an entrance bullet wound to the right cheek and also evidence that firing at the decedent was at close range. Again, the foregoing presents serious issues regarding the deaths of these individuals."

The nine reports and the findings of the independent report would indicate quite conclusively that there was never any intention to take prisoners. Whether the reasons for this—to take out key terrorists and accelerate peace, or to guarantee personal safety and the safety of comrades—justify this is a moot point. However, it is inarguable that the insurgents were not at Loughgall only to surrender to arrest, so it is not surprising that there is no evidence to suggest that any attempts were made to arrest, question or detain any of the men before the attack using the powers of the Emergency Provisions Act and the Prevention of Terrorism Acts.

Sectors of the loyalist community were overjoyed: apparently, soon after the attack triumphalist loyalists painted "'SAS 8 – IRA 0" on the roof of a derelict house in Portadown overlooking the main Dublin–Belfast railway line. Sometime later that night all the SAS and Det soldiers involved were helicoptered out of the province for an unknown period of time.

Surprisingly, Loughgall—operational and propaganda success as it was—did little to affect IRA activity in East Tyrone which did not show any real decline: in the two years before the ambush the IRA killed seven people in East Tyrone and North Armagh, and eleven in the two years following the ambush. It is also worth noting that most of the attacks that took place in County Fermanagh during this time were also launched from south Tyrone and Monaghan. One fact remains, however, and that is that many of the remaining insurgents were young and inexperienced which inevitably led to higher casualties. Altogether, the Provisional IRA East Tyrone Brigade lost fifty-three members during The Troubles, the highest of any rural brigade area. Of these twenty-eight were killed between 1987 and 1992. A former senior IRA figure has said the ranks of the IRA "were flooded" after Loughgall. Not surprisingly this has been disputed with a former RUC Special Branch detective declaring the exact opposite: "They stood the entire brigade down after Loughgall. It totally wrecked them. The witch hunt for a mole destroyed them mentally." Unsurprisingly, many republicans and the men's relatives saw the ambush as part of a deliberate shoot-to-kill policy by the security forces. The funerals were attended by many thousands, creating the biggest republican funerals in Northern Ireland since those of the IRA hunger strikers of 1981. Gerry Adams, in his graveside speech stated that the British government understood that it could buy off the government of the Republic of Ireland, which he described as the "shoneen clan" (pro-British), but added "it does not understand the Jim Lynaghs, the Pádraig McKearneys or the Séamus McElwaines. It thinks it can defeat them. It never will."

An investigation into the deaths at Loughgall was allegedly carried out by the RUC. The families have not been told the contents of the RUC report. On September 22, 1988 the Director of Public Prosecutions announced that no one involved in the shooting at Loughgall was to be prosecuted. The families of the eight IRA men were never informed of this decision.

In June 1995 The Loughgall Truth and Justice campaign representing the nine men killed at Loughgall was formed to search for the truth behind the events of May 8. Their aim was simply for the truth to be told and heard and for those responsible for the nine deaths to be held accountable in a court of law for their actions that evening: "This was a carefully well-planned ambush by the SAS and RUC. They have stated in written documents that they had at least 24 hours prior notice of the IRA's intentions to bomb the unmanned barracks. Intelligence reports show that the British Army and the RUC knew of the IRA's plan to attack the Loughgall RUC barracks, as well as the IRA personnel involved, several weeks in advance, yet no attempt was made whatsoever to arrest or detain these individuals or to prevent the attack from taking place. The Prevention of Terrorism Act and the Emergency Provisions Act give the RUC and army enormous power and discretion to stop, question and search anyone suspected of planning an offence. The British armed forces, sanctioned at the highest level, however, chose not to utilise these extreme investigative authorisations, but instead carried out a shoot-to-kill ambush clearly calculated to murder these known individuals, evidencing a callous indifference for due process and human life in clear contravention of Article 2 of the European Convention of Human Rights."

The Provisional IRA's take on the ambush is summarized: "As revolutionary soldiers we accept that it's blood for blood, like for like, our boys would have done the same to them, but this was a 'shoot-to-kill' policy sanctioned at the highest levels of the state. This was a war. Why did they let the explosives through, they had so many opportunities to stop that operation?" The IRA released a further statement: "...

volunteers who shot their way out of the ambush and escaped saw other volunteers being shot on the ground after being captured."

In 2001 the European Court of Human Rights ruled that ten IRA members, including the eight killed at Loughgall, had their human rights violated by the failure of the British government to conduct a proper investigation into their deaths; there was no suggestion that these deaths amounted to unlawful killing. The court ruled that the British government should pay £10,000 compensation to each of the families of the IRA members killed in the Loughgall incident. In December 2011, Northern Ireland's Historical Enquiries Team established that not only was the IRA team the first to open fire (and not the SAS as originally believed) but that they could never have been safely arrested without loss of life to the security forces. They concluded that the SAS were justified in opening fire.

When asked by the *Daily Mail*'s Peter Taylor, the chief constable of the time, Sir John Hermon, why the ASU could not have been arrested instead of being shot by the SAS, he said that "it was never a realistic option since the IRA would be unlikely to come out with their hands up and police officers lives would therefore be at grave risk." (*Daily Mail* May 5, 2001)

According to declassified papers first published on December 29, 2017, Gerry Adams himself was rumoured to have set up the IRA gang. The rumour was passed on to the department of foreign affairs by a respected cleric, Father Denis Faul, about three months after the Loughgall operation. The priest said the theory doing the rounds was that the IRA team were set up by Gerry Adams himself, a claim hotly denied by Sinn Féin spokesman. Father Faul, a school teacher and chaplain at Long Kesh prison, confirmed that word on the street was that two of the gang—Jim Lynagh, a councillor in Monaghan, and McKearney—"had threatened to execute Adams shortly before the Loughgall event", that they "disliked Adams' political policy" and were leaning toward republican Sinn Féin. The released documents (file 2017/4/74) further reveal that three days after the operation, Tánaiste and foreign affairs minister Brian Lenihan wrote to secretary of state Tom King urging him not to triumph over the killings: "We asked you through the Secretariat to be mindful of the need to avoid any sense of triumphalism on the part of your authorities," he said. "It is necessary that sensitivity be shown in regard to the funerals which are now taking place and that the investigation of the events should pay particular attention to the question of whether such a large number of casualties, including the civilian casualty, could have been avoided." Tom King replied: "My advice is that that [IRA] group had at least 40–50 murders to their score over the years."

Further notes from briefings by the British government to Irish officials in London revealed that the gun battle lasted two to three minutes, that the SAS fired "no more rounds than were necessary" and that every IRA weapon had been fired. In the same file, Bishop of Clogher Joseph Duffy told a diplomat that Lynagh was a "madman" and was believed to have been responsible for twenty murders, including that of Sir Norman Strange and his son in January 1981. In 2015, it was announced that a fresh inquest was to be held.

Military Reaction Force

Few people know for sure what MRF stands for; it is variously given as Military Reaction Force, Military Reconnaissance Force or Mobile Reconnaissance Force. What we do know is that it operated as a covert intelligence-gathering and counterinsurgency unit of the British Army. A former member, and he should know, described it as a "legalized death squad". It came to be during 1971 and operated in its inimitable way until late 1972 or early 1973. MRF teams operated in plainclothes and used false names and civilian (specially armoured) vehicles equipped with two-way radios. On first-name terms only and with no ranks, they came bearing Browning pistols and Sterling submachine guns, and it was their job to find and arrest, or kill, members of the IRA. The MRF also ran double agents in concert with paramilitary groups and operated a number of front companies from which to garner intelligence. In October 1972, the Provisional IRA uncovered and attacked two of these front companies—a mobile laundry service and a massage parlour—actions which hastened the unit's demise.

The MRF was the brainchild of Brigadier Sir Frank Kitson, who had created 'counter gangs' to defeat the Mau Mau in Kenya. He was also the author of two books on counterinsurgency tactics: *Gangs & Counter Gangs* (1960) and *Low Intensity Operations* (1971).

The MRF was split into squads, each of which was led by a senior NCO who had served in the SAS, Special Boat Service (SBS), the Royal Marines or the Parachute Regiment. The unit consisted of up to forty handpicked men and women. The MRF would deploy up to nine soldiers at any one time, with nine more on standby and the others resting. The unit was stationed at Palace Barracks in Hollywood where there was an operations and briefing room, an armoury and space for cars, typically Hillmans and Ford Cortinas with microphones built into their sun visors. MRF members had to be single. It has been asserted that the MRF's purpose was "to draw the Provisional IRA into a shooting war with loyalists in order to distract the IRA from its objective of attacking the Army". In other words, to fuel sectarian violence.

Former MRF members have admitted that the unit shot unarmed people without warning, both IRA and civilians, in breach of the British Army's rules of engagement. They claim they had a list of targets they were ordered to shoot on sight, tactics which apparently had British government backing "as part of a deeper political game". One former member claimed his section shot at least twenty people: "We opened fire at any small group in hard areas ... armed or not ... it didn't matter. He tells how MRF members visited pubs and 'eliminated' IRA members on two occasions. Another, interviewed for the BBC's *Panorama*, said, "We were not there to act like an army unit, we were there to act like a terror group." Attacks were designed to mimic IRA attacks in terms of weaponry and MO. Former members claim they posed as road sweepers, dustmen and even homeless meths-drinkers while carrying out surveillance. The MRF used double agents, known as 'Freds'—republican or loyalist paramilitaries who would work inside paramilitary groups, feeding back information to the MRF. They were ferried around Belfast in armoured cars, and through the gunslit would point-out paramilitary individuals of interest. In 1972, MRF teams carried out a number of drive-by shootings in Catholic areas of Belfast, some of which were pinned on loyalist paramilitaries. At least fifteen civilians were shot. MRF members have confirmed the unit's involvement in many of these attacks. Following are just some of the incidents in which the MRF is alleged to have been involved.

On December 4, 1971, UVF detonated a time bomb at the door of McGurk's public house in Belfast. There are allegations, by a former UVF member, that the MRF organized this and assisted the passage of the bombers in and out of the area, blaming the atrocity on the IRA.

On April 15, 1972, when brothers Gerry and John Conway—both Catholic civilians—were walking along Whiterock Road three men jumped out of a car and opened fire; both brothers were wounded. Witnesses said one of the gunmen returned to the car and spoke into a handset radio and a bit later two armoured personnel carriers arrived, and there was a conversation between the uniformed and the plainclothes soldiers. In 1978 a former MRF member claimed he had been one of the gunmen, that the brothers were unarmed and that his patrol had mistaken the brothers for two IRA men whom the MRF had orders to shoot on sight.

When, on May 2, 1972, the British government announced there would be no disciplinary action against the soldiers involved in 'Bloody Sunday', MRF teams added insult to injury when they shot seven Catholic civilians in the Andersonstown area. The first murder came when am MRF team drove up to a checkpoint manned by members of the Catholic Ex-Servicemen's Association (CESA), an unarmed vigilante organization set up to protect Catholic areas. One of the MRF opened fire from the car with a submachine gun, shot Catholic civilian Patrick McVeigh (44) in the back and wounded four others. An inquest into the attack in December 1972 admitted that the car's occupants were MRF members; the soldiers claimed they were shot at but forensic evidence proved the CESA people were unarmed. No MRF members involved were prosecuted. In 1978 a former member declared that the British Army's intention was to make it look like a loyalist attack to fuel sectarian conflict and "take the heat off the Army". Minutes before this incident Aidan McAloon and Eugene Devlin had taken a taxi home from a disco and were dropped off at Slievegallion Drive when another MRF team shot them; police forensics experts found no evidence that McAloon or Devlin had been armed. On May 27, Catholic civilian Gerard Duddy (20) was murdered in a drive-by shooting at the same spot where Patrick McVeigh was killed. His death was blamed on loyalists.

The night of June 9, 1972 saw the execution of Catholic civilian Jean Smyth-Campbell, a twenty-four-year-old mother, on the Glen Road. The car in which Smyth-Campbell was an innocent passenger was sprayed with automatic gunfire: she was shot in the head and died soon afterward. When the driver hailed a passing cab to take her to hospital the taxi was stopped by police and diverted to Andersonstown RUC base where it was detained for several hours. The security forces blamed the killing on the IRA but in October 1973 the *Belfast Telegraph* suggested that Smyth-Campbell could have been shot by the MRF. National Archives documents reveal that the MRF fired shots in the area that night. The *Telegraph* article also suggested that Smyth-Campbell could have been shot by the IRA who fired on the car thinking it was carrying MRF members. The IRA deny this.

On June 22, 1972, MRF members in an unmarked car shot and wounded three Catholic men; the MRF car was stopped by the RUC and the occupants arrested in possession of a Thompson submachine gun. One of the MRF members—Clive Graham Williams—was charged with attempted murder; he later told the court that two of the men had been armed, and one had fired at the MRF car. Police forensics experts found no evidence that the civilians had fired weapons. Key witnesses were not called to give evidence in person. Williams was acquitted on June 26, 1973 and was later promoted and awarded the Military Medal for bravery.

The MRF was allegedly involved in a drive-by shooting in the Catholic New Lodge area on February 3, 1973 when the car's occupants opened fire on a group of young people standing outside a pub on Antrim Road, killing IRA members James Sloan and James McCann and wounding others. The gunmen drove on and allegedly fired at another group of people outside a takeaway. In the hours that followed, a further four people—an IRA member and three civilians—were shot dead in the same area by British snipers.

Four Square Laundry was a mobile laundry service operating in nationalist west Belfast; the Gemini Health Studios massage parlour was on the Antrim Road. The MRF also had an office at College Square. All were designed to gather intelligence on the Provisional IRA. A Four Square van would visit houses twice a week to collect and deliver laundry. A man drove the van while a young woman collected and delivered the laundry. Clothes collected for washing were forensically checked for traces of explosives, as well as blood or firearms residue. They were also compared to previous laundry loads from the same house: the sudden presence of different-sized clothes could indicate that the house was harbouring an insurgent. Surveillance operatives and equipment were hidden in the van; additional intelligence was gathered by chatting to locals while collecting their laundry.

In September 1972 the IRA discovered that two of its members—Seamus Wright and Kevin McKee—were working for the MRF as double agents. Under interrogation, McKee told the IRA about the MRF's operations, including the laundry and the massage parlour. The companies were put under surveillance which confirmed that McKee's information was correct. The IRA later took Wright and McKee to South Armagh, where they were executed as spies. Their bodies were recovered in 2015. But the IRA was far from finished. On October 2, 1972 the 2nd Battalion of the Belfast Brigade was detailed to attack the Four Square Laundry van and the office at College Square, while the 3rd Battalion would raid the massage parlour. IRA volunteers ambushed the Four Square Laundry van, shot dead the driver, an undercover British soldier of the Royal Engineers, and machine-gunned the roof compartment where undercover operatives were thought to be hiding. The IRA claimed to have killed two surveillance officers allegedly hidden in the van. Bizarrely, the female operative from the Women's Royal Army Corps (WRAC) who was collecting and delivering laundry from a nearby house at the time was taken in by residents who thought that loyalists were attacking the van. She was later secretly invested at Buckingham Palace with an MBE.

An hour later, the College Square office was raided but there was nobody in. A unit of the 3rd Battalion attacked the massage parlour where they claim to have shot three undercover soldiers: two men and a woman. Whatever the real death toll, the MRF cover was blown and the unit disbanded. In November 1972, a review of the MRF ordered by the army found there was "no provision for detailed command and control". The MRF was succeeded by the Det, the Special Reconnaissance Unit (SRU) or 14 Intelligence Company and, later, by the Force Research Unit (FRU). Interestingly, Prime Minister Edward Heath told the army that "special care should be taken" to ensure that the new unit should "operate within the law".

The MRF often clearly acted outside the British Army's rules of engagement and the famous Yellow Card was rarely in evidence, it seems. According to journalist John Ware in the *Irish Republican News* of November 23, 2013, "These baiting tactics were outside the rules governing the use of lethal force known as the Yellow Card, which required a soldier to challenge a gunman, offering him the chance to put down his weapon before opening fire—unless the soldier felt his life was in imminent danger. In the real world of Belfast 1972, one man with a gun confronted by another was only ever going to end one way. All of the MRF soldiers we spoke to say they often ignored the Yellow Card. 'If we didn't do what we did, nothing was going to get done,' said Soldier H. As to 'death squads'—a label paradoxically shared by nationalists with long memories and one of the two former MRF soldiers turned author—Soldier D said: 'I totally reject "death squad,"' only to pause and add: 'Put yourself in my situation: we've got a dirty war, a war that was out of control. We knew who the operators were, we knew who the shooters were. So what are you going to do about it, John?'"

Special Reconnaissance Unit, 14 Field Security & Intelligence Company

"From 1974 to 1978 the Det pioneered how surveillance could be conducted ... the basics early Det operators established revolutionized surveillance."

William Matchett, *Secret Victory: The Intelligence War That Beat the IRA*

Matchett's quote is matched by James Rennie in *The Operators: On the Streets with Britain's Most Secret Service*: "The selection process is the most physically, intellectually and emotionally demanding anywhere in the world." So too Peter Taylor in *Brits: The War Against the IRA*: "It was intelligence-gathering of the most sophisticated and dangerous kind ... in terms of results, a single 'operator' was said to be worth a Company of a hundred regular soldiers."

After the MRF débâcle it was deemed vital to install a replacement unit in the province that should be a specialist force of highly trained, plainclothes surveillance operatives. 14 Intelligence Company was to be recruited and trained by a specially formed training wing of 22 SAS; SAS officers would make up some of the unit's command. In 1973, three detachments, or 'dets' were set up, each within its own sector of Northern Ireland. A depot at Pontrilas near Hereford equipped with various facilities used in counterterrorism (CT) and assault training was complemented by four operational detachments in Northern Ireland: Main Det (Headquarters) at RAF Aldergrove, East Det at Palace Barracks in Belfast, North Det at Balykelly, County Derry and South Det based in Fermanagh. The first deployment was 120 men and women. Initially, when posted to Det it was to NITAT, the innocuous sounding Northern Ireland Training Advisory Team.

Troops from the SAS and SBS would serve two-year tours with 14 Company; selection was later extended to other army units, notably the Royal Corps of Signals. After a tour, the Det soldiers went back to their original regiments for two years, after which they were eligible to return to the Det for another tour. Serving with the Det brought with it invaluable and unique experience that would not only enhance their assigned Det with their particular skills sets, but the operatives would return to their units with priceless operational experience.

Selection to 14 Company was open to all members, men and women, of the armed services who had served for two years. Candidates were required to pass a very rigorous SAS selection process and demonstrate excellence in observational abilities,

Selections are held twice yearly, in summer and winter in Sennybridge and in the Brecon Beacons. Selection normally starts with about 200 potential candidates. Upon arrival candidates first complete a Personal Fitness Test (PFT) and an Annual Fitness Test (AFT). They then march cross-country against the clock, increasing the distances covered each day, culminating in what is known as Endurance. This is a march of 40 miles with full equipment, scaling and descending Pen y Fan (pictured) inside 20 hours. By the end of the hill phase candidates must be able to run 4 miles in 30 minutes and swim two miles in 90 minutes or less.

phenomenal stamina and the ability to think, operate and make decisive judgements under extreme stress—all vital for undercover surveillance work.

Proven confidence and self-reliance were other prerequisites. Of the 300 selected for training in one of the early programmes, only seventeen made it to Northern Ireland.

Candidates reported for training carrying nothing that would reveal rank or unit; diaries and address books were confiscated. Sleep-deprived mental powers were tested to the extreme; thunder flashes were dropped down chimneys in the middle of the night and trainees had to extract themselves from the billet in the dark. 'Milling' was where a candidate would have to box to exhaustion with a colleague in the middle of the night. Kim's Game was another nocturnal activity in which up to seventy mundane articles were displayed and the trainee had to recall them all. Extensive car training included advanced driving courses with sustained high-speed driving, using a vehicle as a weapon, controlled crashes, skid recovery and anti-ambush skills.

Aptitude in photography was essential: candidates first learned the basics then graduated to advanced nighttime, infrared photography. They also became adept at concealing still and video cameras in their clothing and in cars. Obviously, the disciplines of surveillance—from hiding in ditches or attics, to following on foot, to surveillance from vehicles—were all driven home as was the ability to patiently observe, follow and communicate over the radio network, all covertly. Operators were also taught how to plant electronic eavesdropping devices, or bugs, in homes, businesses and arms caches, to install and use covert video cameras and work tracking devices on suspect cars and even on people—'jarking' in army parlance. Housebreaking and breaking into businesses to plant bugs and gathering intelligence were also learned, as were lock-picking and key-copying.

The ideal was to avoid direct contact with targets but that was not always possible. Det members had to be highly skilled in close quarters combat (CQC). Proficiency in unarmed combat was essential, particularly techniques to effectively disarm and neutralize knife- or gun-wielding assailants.

Body language technique was practised to enable the operators to melt into the environment in which they were working. Inconspicuous dress was essential, as were hairstyles.

There were particularly arduous courses on how to act if captured, interrogated and tortured before, inevitably, being executed. Men and women would be sleep-deprived, stripped naked, doused in cold water, abused physically and verbally, and assaulted.

Members became expert pistol users, usually on Browning Hi-Powers or the smaller Walther PPKs, with proficiency also in the use of submachine guns such as HK MP5ks,

HK53 carbines and G3KA4 assault rifles. They were trained in deploying their weapons from within their vehicles as part of anti-ambush drills. Det operatives would usually have an extra pistol—often another Browning HP with an extended twenty-round magazine—concealed in their vehicles. A Remington 870 shotgun was also hidden inside Det cars; this was used to blast out the windscreens of their vehicles, allowing the operatives inside to fire their other weapons from within. Operators wore microphones and earphones hidden in their clothing to enable them to talk on 'the net' while in public. Special covert holsters allowed an operators to conceal a pistol in their waistbands or on their ankles.

They drove a range of cars, Q cars, which to all intents and purposes looked like every-day civilian saloons—Ford Sierras, VW Passats and Audis, for example—but in fact were full of 'extras': covert radios with hidden speakers and microphones that could not be spotted from the outside came as standard as were video and still cameras; brake lights could easily be disabled so as to allow them to covertly pick up or drop off operatives at night; engine cut-off switches were fitted as a hijacking countermeasure; cars were fitted with systems to detect any tampering with the vehicle;s electronics—a sure sign that a car bomb had been introduced. Q cars were fitted with covert kevlar armour plating. Discreet gaps were left in the armour to allow operatives to fire through the bodywork—useful in ambushes. Flashbang dispensers were secreted beneath Q cars which when triggered by a footswitch detonated multiple stun grenades that would fly out in all directions before detonating. Again, indispensable for extricating from terrorist roadblocks or for dispersing a hostile crowd.

Fittingly, the unit went by a myriad of names designed to confuse: 14th Intelligence Detachment, Northern Ireland Training and Advisory Teams (Northern Ireland) or NITAT(NI), Intelligence and Security Group (NI), Int & Sy Group, 14 Intelligence and Security Company, 14 Intelligence Company, 14 Company, 14 Int, The Det, Special Reconnaissance Unit, The Unit and The Watchers.

Det had access to a flight of Army Air Corps (AAC) Gazelles, nicknamed the 'Bat flight', for operations. These Gazelles were, of course, fitted with highly sophisticated surveillance equipment. Video and Forward Looking Infrared (FLIR) cameras were slaved to a sight usually used to fire wire-guided missiles. It was practice for at least one Det operator to ride in the helicopter and track suspects through the sighting system, usually high up, out of sight and earshot.

Det's painstaking intelligence-gathering led to the arrest of numerous terrorists by the RUC as well as the discovery of many a weapons cache. They liaised closely with SAS teams, acting as their eyes and ears and providing covert transportation for SAS operations. Allegations of collusion with loyalist terrorists came with their alleged involvement in the death of senior Provisional IRA member John Francis Green, the Miami Showband killings and the Dublin and Monaghan bombings.

Occasionally Det members got embroiled in firefights with terrorists; several 14 Company operators lost their lives as a result:

In April 1974 Captain Anthony Pollen (27) was murdered in Derry while carrying out undercover surveillance on a Sinn Féin march. He was shot twice in front of a crowd of more than 150 people. On May 15, 1977 Captain Robert Nairac (29) was kidnapped in Silverbridge, County Armagh and shot by the IRA. His body remains undiscovered. On December 14, 1977 Corporal Paul Harman (27) was executed by the IRA in west Belfast. Harman was undercover when he pulled up his red Morris Marina on Monagh Avenue. An IRA unit approached the car and shot him in the head and back, stole his weapon and intelligence files, radio codebooks, and torched the car. On August 11, 1978: Lance-Corporal Alan Swift (25) was shot dead while undercover, parked up in the Bogside area of Derry. Two IRA members fired into the corporal's car with automatic rifles from a Toyota van. On May 6, 1979 Sergeant Robert Maughan was shot dead outside a church in Lisnaskea. On February 21, 1984 Sergeant Paul Oram (26) was killed in an incident in mainly nationalist Dunloy, Ballymoney, when he and a colleague were surprised in the dead of night by an IRA unit operating in the area. Oram and his colleague drew their pistols and engaged but Oram was killed instantly. According to his colleague, the two IRA members collapsed, wounded, but he shot and killed them as, in his opinion, they still constituted a threat. Oram's colleague was seriously wounded but team-members patrolling nearby assisted, and he survived.

On March 19, 1988 corporals David Howes and Derek Wood inadvertently drove into the funeral procession in Andersonstown of Caoimhín Mac Brádaigh. Prevented from escape by black taxis, the soldiers were dragged from their armoured car, a silver Volkswagen Passat hatchback, stripped and found to be armed. They were taken away and shot by the Provisional IRA. The so-called Corporals' Killings have been described earlier but the testimony of Father Alec Reid—later a significant figure in the peace process, is worthwhile repeating: "I got down between the two of them and I had my arm around this one and I was holding this one up by the shoulder," he recalled. "They were so disciplined, they just lay there totally still and I decided to myself they were soldiers. There was a helicopter circling overhead and I don't know why they didn't do something, radio to the police or soldiers to come up, because there were these two of their own soldiers," he added. "When I was lying between the two soldiers, I remember saying to myself, 'This shouldn't be happening in a civilized society.' That motivated me or encouraged me to keep trying to get away from this kind of society where this kind of thing could happen." He said he kept asking people at the scene to call an ambulance. "I was lying there and I saw someone came in. [He] picked me up and said, 'Get up or I will f***ing well shoot you as well.' And then he said, 'Take him away' and they kind of arrested me. Two of them came on either shoulder and kind of manoeuvred me off ... then I got around and came back ... I can still remember the atmosphere. When I came back in, you could feel it; I knew they were going to be shot ... I remember saying to myself I am going to try and stop them doing that if I can." The corporals were then driven to waste ground near Casement Park. Father Reid said he decided to follow them and as he was getting into his car he heard two shots. He then went on to the waste ground where the soldiers lay. "There was nobody else there, just the two bodies. I went up to the one on the right. He was still breathing so I tried to give him the kiss of life. Then after a while a man came in and stood behind me and said, 'Look, Father, that man is dead.' I anointed him and went over to anoint the man who was lying three yards away. Then two women came along with a coat and put it over his head and said, 'He was somebody's son.'

"I felt I had done my best to save them. I was very shocked and I felt bad—I had failed to save them and that was the bottom line."

Reporter Gerry Moriarty adds: "Even amid the despair there was some hope, as at the time Father Reid was carrying correspondence between the Sinn Féin president Gerry Adams and SDLP leader John Hume. This was part of the initial exchanges between the SDLP and Sinn Féin leaders that led to the Hume–Adams talks and the subsequent IRA ceasefire of 1994."

Corporals Derek Wood (24) and David Howes (23), both Royal Corps of Signals.

The terrible events were observed by an army surveillance Gazelle helicopter, its live feed relayed back to the Det control room where the corporals' colleagues were watching in real-time horror. Allegedly, one of these operatives was the girlfriend of one of the corporals; the footage was later produced in evidence at a series of trials related to the incident. The army explanation was that the soldiers were Royal Corps of Signals technicians, engaged in routine communications work at bases in West Belfast but it was suspected that the corporals were indeed involved in undercover surveillance. To this day, however, no one knows why a highly trained Det patrol got so embroiled in a funeral attended by hundreds of republican sympathizers. An 'out-of-bounds area' would have been issued to all units, but fatally the corporals strayed into 'the box'.

This is the IRA's statement: "The Belfast brigade, IRA, claims responsibility for the execution of two SAS members who launched an attack on the funeral cortège of our comrade volunteer Kevin Brady. The SAS unit was initially apprehended by the people lining the route in the belief that armed loyalists were attacking them and they were removed from the immediate vicinity. Our volunteers forcibly removed the two men from the crowd and, after clearly ascertaining their identities from equipment and documentation, we executed them."

The documentation included a security pass with Herford printed on it; Herford is a BAOR base in Germany and was presumably confused by the IRA with Hereford. The shootings led to the largest criminal investigation in Northern Ireland's history, but simply exacerbated tensions. More than two hundred people were arrested in connection with the killings over four years, of whom forty-one were charged with a variety of offences. The first of these so-called Casement Trials concluded quickly: two men were found guilty of murder and given life sentences. Of the trials that followed, many were based on weaker evidence and proved rather more controversial. (There is a postscript to the attack: on August 2, 1988, Lance-Corporal Roy Butler of the Ulster Defence Regiment was shot and killed in Belfast with one of the guns taken from the corporals.)

For their part, Det operatives were responsible for the following killings: on December 12, 1977 Colm McNutt (18), an INLA leader, was shot dead in Derry City when attempting to hijack at gunpoint a Det vehicle. On June 10, 1978 in Derry Denis Heaney (28) was shot dead by a Det operative when, with a colleague, he attempted to hijack his car. His weapon was recovered at the scene. On May 28, 1981 Charles Maguire (21) and George McBrearty (23) were shot by the Det in a Derry City ambush; two automatic rifles were recovered from the scene. On February 2, 1983 Neil McMonagle (23) confronted a Det operator with another man and was shot dead, in Coshquin, County Derry. On February 21, 1984 when Henry Hogan (21) and Declan Martin (18) tried to ambush a Det observation post (OP) they were shot dead. Det operator Paul Hogan died here too. On September 2, 1989 Brian Robinson (27), a UVF member, was shot dead by the Det in North Belfast in an incident in which a Catholic was murdered; another UVF member was injured and received a life sentence for murder. On January 13, 1990 three members of a gang—Peter Thompson (21), Edward Hale (25) and John McNeill—were shot dead by the Det in the throes of an armed robbery at Sean Graham's bookmakers. Two were wearing balaclavas and brandishing imitation weapons; real weapons were recovered at the scene. The getaway driver was unarmed. The inquest jury found unlawful killing.

Force Research Unit & MI5

The Force Research Unit (FRU) was another covert military intelligence unit of the British Army, part of the Intelligence Corps. It was established in 1982 specifically to obtain intelligence by penetrating terrorist organizations in Northern Ireland by recruiting and running agents and informants. It worked alongside existing intelligence agencies: the RUC Special Branch—who considered the unit to be "rubbish"—and, hovering in the background, MI5. Indeed, the FRU was found conclusively to have colluded with British loyalist paramilitaries in the murder of civilians. This has been confirmed by some former members of the unit.

In the mid-1980s, a man called Brian Nelson was pivotal in the FRU. That man, a former British soldier, was also known as Agent 6137: he was on the payroll of MI5 and planted, by the FRU, into the Ulster Defence Association. In the first seventeen months, Nelson met his handlers around sixty times and received more than £2,000 in cash payments. With FRU help Nelson rose to become the UDA's chief intelligence officer. In 1988 he organized weapons shipments to loyalists through a deal with Armscor, an apartheid South Africa's arms corporation. Nelson was particularly keen on an automatic shotgun called the Striker which "could be used to devastating effect ... in close-quarter combat". Armscor was happy with a cash sale for the guns but, for their part, also wanted to know whether the UDA could supply one of the latest generation of ground-to-air missiles in development at Shorts in east Belfast.

Two years later, Armscor provided weapons to loyalist paramilitaries in a trafficking operation that was paid for by a £325,000 robbery from a bank in Portadown. Armscor's European agent had learned that a large cache of arms held by a Lebanese militia group in Beirut was on the market. The arms were procured and loaded into a container then shipped to Belfast via Liverpool, complete with bills of lading and notes of origin that indicated the cargo was ceramic floor tiles. "There were at least a couple of hundred Czech-made AKs, more than 90 Browning-type handguns, Hungarian-made P9Ms and about 30,000 rounds of ammunition plus a dozen

Springfield Road, west Belfast 'Usual Suspects' mural.

or so RPGs and a few hundred fragmentation grenades," recalls a former Armscor employee who helped broker the deal. At every step of the way, this source says, the UDA's intelligence officer—Agent 6137—was kept informed of its progress. The 'tiles' were unloaded at Belfast docks in late December and smuggled into the country undetected. In January the arsenal was divided three ways at a farmhouse in County Armagh between the UDA, the UVF and a third loyalist paramilitary group, Ulster Resistance. The consequences of this successful gun-running were profound. Loyalists' access to high-grade weapons was enhanced no end as was their ability to slaughter both republicans and uninvolved Catholics. In the six years before the importation of the South African weapons, from January 1982 to December 1987, loyalists murdered seventy-one people. In the seven years after, from January 1988 to September 1, 1994, loyalists killed 229 people. Today, loyalists maintain that the IRA was forced to sue for peace because of the pressure it came under from the killings in the aftermath of the South African smuggling operation. Nelson it was who helped the UDA with assassination targets, passing "Intelligence Packages" including backgrounds, addresses, photos and movements on proposed targets, to UDA assassins. The Stevens Inquiry team found that Nelson was responsible for at least thirty murders and many other attacks; many of the victims were uninvolved civilians.

By the end of 1985 Nelson had had enough and found work in a small Bavarian town fitting floors in new buildings. In February 1987, however, he received a call from the FRU requesting a meeting. He was flown to Heathrow, where he met an FRU agent-handler and an MI5 officer; between them they persuaded Nelson to return to Belfast and rejoin the UDA as a British agent. He was promised a deposit to buy a new house, a car to enable him to work as a taxi driver, and £200 a week plus generous bonuses. Nelson was earning more money in Germany but he agreed and, until his arrest in January 1990, was paid £46,428 from FRU (taxpayers') funds. MI5 would later tell an official inquiry that it opposed Nelson's re-recruitment.

Nelson used a rudimentary but effective blue card index system from which he would select information on individuals, in effect choosing the people who were to be shot. Four at least, including solicitor Pat Finucane, are known to have been shot dead. Many of the cards had police photographs attached. Much of the information on the cards was supplied by the FRU. In Stevens's words, "the FRU had been inexcusably careless in failing to protect the four who lost their lives". Nelson doled out his blue cards, twenty and fifty at a time, to members of the UVF. Many loyalists never bothered to destroy the cards, however, gifting the Stevens team fingerprint evidence. As well as the information supplied by the FRU, Nelson and other members of the UDA were getting material from other soldiers and police officers. In the mid-1980s, MI5 estimated that 85% of the UDA's intelligence was the result of security force leaks. The largest single source was the UDR. At his trial in 1992 the prosecution alleged that Nelson failed to alert his handlers to all the assassination plans of which he was aware. It was counter-claimed that Nelson had warned the Intelligence Corps of more than 200 murder plots by loyalist death squads, including one which targeted Sinn Féin leader Gerry Adams and that Nelson's warnings allowed the British Army to prevent all 200 murders but three. The Stevens Inquiry found evidence that only two lives were saved and said many loyalist attacks could have been prevented but were allowed to go ahead.

Nelson claimed that, in 1989, he had warned his handlers of UDA plans to murder solicitor Pat Finucane. Patrick Finucane (1949–89) was an Irish human rights lawyer killed by loyalist paramilitaries acting in collusion with MI5. Finucane had successfully challenged the British government in several important human rights cases during the 1980s. For his troubles he was shot fourteen times as he sat eating a meal at his Belfast home with his wife and three children. In September 2004, a UDA member, and a paid informant for the Royal Ulster Constabulary, Ken Barrett, pleaded guilty to his murder. Finucane was slaughtered at his home in Fortwilliam Drive, north Belfast, by Ken Barrett, a former policeman, and another masked man using a Browning HP 9mm pistol and a .38 revolver. He was hit multiple times. The two gunmen battered down the front door with a sledgehammer and entered the kitchen where Finucane was having Sunday dinner with his family. The shooting began just as Finucane's wife, Geraldine, reached out to press an alarm button. The opening shots hit him twice in the chest, knocking him to the floor. Then standing over him, his dining fork still in his left hand, the leading gunman fired twelve bullets into him at close range: six times in the head, three times in the neck and three times in the torso. "His face was heavily covered in powder burns, which indicated that he had been shot several times at a range not greater than 15 inches." Geraldine Finucane was slightly wounded in the attack which their three children witnessed as they hid under the table.

Two public investigations have concluded that British security forces colluded in Finucane's murder and there have been high-profile calls for a public inquiry. An independent judge, Peter Cory, of the Canadian supreme court, concluded that he had seen 'strong evidence' of collusive acts by the FRU, RUC Special Branch and

Remembering Pat Finucane.

MI5. However, in October 2011, it was announced that a planned independent public inquiry would be replaced by a less exhaustive review. This review, led by Desmond Lorenz de Silva, released a report in December 2012 that acknowledged that the case entailed "a wilful and abject failure by successive Governments". Finucane's family labelled the De Silva Report a "sham" and a "suppression of the truth" into which they were allowed no input. In June 2007, it was reported that no police or soldiers would be charged in connection with the killing. David Cameron, when prime minister, has since offered an apology for the errant collusion between the then British government and loyalists.

Pat Finucane could count amongst his clients IRA hunger striker Bobby Sands along with other IRA and INLA hunger strikers who died during the 1981 Maze Prison protest, Brian Gillen and the widow of Gervaise McKerr, one of three men shot dead by the RUC in a shoot-to-kill incident in 1982. In 1988, he represented Pat McGeown who was charged in connection with the Corporals' Killings, and was photographed with McGeown outside Crumlin Road courthouse. Finucane had also represented loyalists. Some within the British Army clearly believed Finucane to be a member of the IRA: he appeared within the records of the Northern Ireland headquarters as 'Patrick Finucane, RC, 21 Mar 49(D) PIRA P2327'. MI5 had no time for him and set about spreading chatter which had him down as a terrorist, part of what MI5 called a counteraction campaign designed to "unnerve" such individuals and ensure that the rumours reached loyalist paramilitaries looking for targets and revenge. Eventually Nelson pleaded guilty to twenty charges, including five of conspiracy to murder and was sentenced to ten years' imprisonment. A number of charges, including two counts of first-degree murder, were dropped as part of his plea bargain.

Finucane's law firm, Madden & Finucane Solicitors continues to act for those it considers to have been victims of mistreatment by the state, or their survivors. The Pat Finucane Centre (PFC), named in his honour, is a human rights advocacy and lobbying entity in Northern Ireland.

Even after Nelson was imprisoned in 1992, FRU intelligence continued to help the UDA and other loyalist groups. From 1992 to 1994, loyalists were responsible for more deaths than republicans for the first time since the 1960s. After more than thirteen years investigating state-sponsored death squads, collusion between the British state and the terrorists it was supposed to be combating, Stevens's third and final report was completed. So far, his work had led to the conviction of ninety-four people. None of them was from the FRU, RUC Special Branch or MI5. On the contrary, the FRU's commanding officer was promoted, as was Nelson's main handler who was also decorated.

In an extract from *The History Thieves: Secrets, Lies and the Shaping of a Modern Nation* by Ian Cobain published in *The Irish Times*, September 19, 2016 we learn that,

"In the course of their investigation, Stevens' team had taken 9,256 statements and gathered 10,391 documents, totalling more than a million pages, not counting those lost in the fire at Seapark in Carrickfergus. His final report ran to several thousand pages. Just nineteen of those pages were made public ... the documents that his team had amassed were estimated to weigh around 100 tonnes." It was also alleged that the FRU had routinely applied for restriction orders on a number of loyalist paramilitary attacks in order to facilitate access to and expedite escape from their target. A restriction order was a de-confliction agreement to restrict patrolling or surveillance in an area over a specified period carried out at a weekly Tasking and Co-ordination Group that included representatives of the Royal Ulster Constabulary, MI5 and the British Army.

The FRU is also alleged to have handled agents embedded within republican paramilitary groups including active and lethal IRA units. The most notorious agent went by the codename 'Stakeknife', possibly IRA member Freddie Scappaticci. Stakeknife was probably a member of the IRA's Internal Security Unit, or 'Nutting Squad', responsible for counterintelligence, interrogation and court martial of informers within the IRA. He was allegedly used by the FRU to influence the outcome of investigations conducted by the Internal Security Unit. It is alleged that he was being paid at least £80,000 a year and had a bank account in Gibraltar. It is further alleged that the British government permitted up to forty people to be killed by the Internal Security Unit in order to protect his cover. An IRA source quoted in *The Guardian*, May 12, 2003, said: "He was the bogeyman of the IRA: judge, jury and executioner. He didn't have to attend brigade meetings. He didn't get involved in the politics or talking. But whenever something went wrong, Freddy Scappaticci was sent for." The article continues: "But this man, entrusted by the IRA army council with a crucial role, was in fact the British Army's most precious asset at the heart of the republican movement for a quarter of a century."

When the FRU discovered that Stakeknife was likely to be assassinated by the UDA, they tasked Brian Nelson with persuading the UDA to assassinate Francisco Notarantonio instead, a Belfast pensioner who had been interned as an Irish republican in the 1940s. The killing of Notarantonio was claimed by the UFF at the time; the IRA assassinated two UDA leaders in reprisal attacks. Allegedly the FRU secretly passed details of the two UDA leaders to the IRA via Stakeknife to divert attention from Stakeknife as a possible informer.

Former FRU operative Martin Ingram has stated that the arson attack that destroyed the offices of the Stevens Inquiry was carried out by the FRU to destroy evidence on operational activities collected by Stevens's team. Fire-safety equipment, fire alarms and phone lines in the high-security facility in Carrickfergus were disabled. Luckily,

The funeral of Martin McGuiness, March 23, 2017. James Martin Pacelli McGuinness was an Irish republican and Sinn Féin politician and deputy First Minister of Northern Ireland from May 2007 to January 2017. A former IRA leader, McGuinness was the MP for Mid Ulster from 1997 until his resignation in 2013.

a 'duplicate office' had been set up at the headquarters of the Cambridgeshire police. Later, Stevens looked back on his investigation declaring that "in almost thirty years as a policeman I had never found myself caught up in such an entanglement of lies and treachery". Stevens disclosed that of the 210 people his team arrested, only three were not agents of the British state. Some were working simultaneously for the police, the Army, MI5 and, he hinted, MI6. All were making large sums of money, frequently while fighting against each other, "which was all against the public interest and creating mayhem in Northern Ireland".

Cobain goes on to tell us by April 2014 the average time that families had been waiting for an adjourned inquest to be concluded was twenty years and seven months. Almost all concerned killings by police officers or soldiers, or by loyalist paramilitaries who were suspected of being state agents. And so it went.

Further Reading

14 Company ('The Det') www.eliteukforces.info/the-det/

Adams, J., Morgan, R. & Bainbridge, A., *Ambush: The War between the SAS and the IRA*, Pan, London 1988

Asher, M., *Shoot to Kill: A Soldier's Journey Through Violence*, Penguin, London 1991

Barberis, P. (ed.), *Encyclopedia of British and Irish Political Organizations*, Continuum, London 2000

Baron Hunt (Hunt, John), 'Report of The Advisory Committee on Police in Northern Ireland', Belfast 1969

Bell, J., *The Irish Troubles: A Generation of Violence, 1967–1992*, St. Martin's Press, London 1993

Bennett, H., 'The reluctant pupil? Britain's army and learning in counter-insurgency', Royal United Services Institute 2009

Beresford, D., *Ten Men Dead: The Story of the 1981 Irish Hunger Strike*, Hunter Publishing, West Palm Beach, FLA 1989

Bishop, P. & Mallie, E., *The Provisional IRA*, Corgi, London 1988

Bonner, D., *Executive Measures, Terrorism and National Security: Have the Rules of the Game Changed?*, Routledge, London 2016

Borthwick, S., *The Writing on the Wall: A Visual History of Northern Ireland's Troubles*, The Bluecoat Press, Liverpool 2015

Boulton, D., *UVF 1966–1973: An Anatomy of Loyalist Rebellion*, Torc 1973

Bruce, S., *The Red Hand: Protestant Paramilitaries in Ulster*, Oxford Paperbacks, Oxford 1992

Cadwallader, A., *Lethal Allies: British Collusion in Ireland*, Mercier Press, Cork 2013

Cassel, D., 'Report of the Independent International Panel on Alleged Collusion in Sectarian Killings in Northern Ireland' (The Cassel Report), Center for Civil and Human Rights, Notre Dame Law School 2006

Charters, D. A., 'Counter-insurgency Intelligence: The Evolution of British Theory and Practice', *The Journal of Conflict Studies* No. 29 2009

Cobain, Ian, *The History Thieves: Secrets, Lies and the Shaping of a Modern Nation*, Portobello Books, London 2016

Collins, E. & McGovern, M., *Killing Rage*, Granta, London 1999

'Collusion in the South Armagh / Mid Ulster Area in the mid-1970s', Pat Finucane Centre 2011, retrieved 31 January 2018; https://web.archive.org/web/20110426121606/http://www.patfinucanecentre.org/sarmagh/sarmagh.html

Committee on the Administration of Justice, 'The Stalker Affair: More Questions than Answers', Belfast 1988

Connor, K., *Ghost Force: Secret History of the SAS*, Orion, London 1999

Coogan, T. P., *The IRA* (5th ed.), Palgrave MacMillan, New York 2002

Crawford, C., *Inside the UDA: Volunteers and Violence*, Pluto Press, London 2003

Cusack, J. & McDonald, H., *UVF*, Poolbeg Press, Dublin 1997

Dillon, M., *God and the Gun: the Church and Irish Terrorism*, Orion, New York 1997

_____, *Political Murder in Northern Ireland*, Penguin, London 1973

_____, *Stone Cold: The True Story of Michael Stone and the Milltown Massacre*, Arrow, London 1993

_____, *The Dirty War*, Arrow, London 1991

_____, *The Shankill Butchers: A Case Study of Mass Murder*, Arrow, London 1990

_____, *The Shankill Butchers: The Real Story of Cold-blooded Mass Murder*, Routledge, New York 1999

Doherty, D., *The Stalker Affair: Including an Account of British Service Operations in Ireland*, Mercier Press, Cork 1986

Doherty, R., *The Thin Green Line: The History of the Royal Ulster Constabulary GC, 1922–2001*, Pen & Sword, Barnsley 2012

Eckert, N., *Fatal Encounter: The Story of the Gibraltar Killings*, Poolbeg Press, Dublin 1999

Edwards, A., *UVF: Behind the Mask*, Merrion Press, Dublin 2017

Edwards, R., *The Faithful Tribe: An Intimate Portrait of the Loyal Institutions*, HarperCollins, London 2000

Ellison, G., *The Crowned Harp: Policing Northern Ireland*, Pluto Press, London 2000

English, R., *Armed Struggle: The History of the IRA* (revised ed.), Pan; Reprints edition, London 2012

Ford, S., *One Up: A Woman in Action with the SAS*, HarperCollins, London 1997

Garland, R., *Gusty Spence*, Blackstaff Press, Belfast 2001

George, J. & Ottoway, S, *She Who Dared: Covert Operations in Northern Ireland with the SAS*, Leo Cooper, Barnsley, 1999

Geraghty, T., *The Irish War*, HarperCollins, London 2000

Griffin, T., 'The long shadow of the Military Reaction Force', spinwatch.org, retrieved January 31, 2018

Harkin, G. & Ingram M., *Stakeknife: Britain's Secret Agents in Ireland*, O'Brien Press, Dublin 2004

Harnden, T., *Bandit Country: The IRA and South Armagh*, Hodder, London 2000

Hennessey, T., *Northern Ireland: The Origin of the Troubles*, Gill & Macmillan, Dublin 2005

Kerr, R., *Republican Belfast: A Political Tourist's Guide*, MSF Press, Belfast 2008

_____, *The Belfast Mural Guide* (2nd revised edition), MSF Press, Belfast 2015

Kiely, D. M., *Deadlier Than the Male: Ireland's Female Killers*, Gill & Macmillan, Dublin 2005

Kitson, F., *Low Intensity Operations: Subversion, Insurgency and Peacekeeping*, Faber & Faber, London 1972

Larkin, P., *A Very British Jihad: Collusion, Conspiracy and Cover-up in Northern Ireland*, Beyond the Pale, Belfast 2004

Lindsay, J., *Brits Speak Out: British Soldiers' Impressions of the Northern Ireland Conflict*, Guildhall Press, Derry 1998

MacAirt, C. *The McGurk's Bar Bombing: Collusion, Cover-Up and a Campaign for Truth*, Frontline Noir, Dublin 2013

Mallie, E. & McKittrick, D., *The Fight for Peace: The Secret Story Behind the Irish Peace Process*, Mandarin 1997

Matchett, W., *Secret Victory: The Intelligence War That Beat the IRA*, Matchett, Belfast 2016

McCaffrey, Barry, 'Revealed—how British threatened harsh sanctions over SAS arrests', *Irish News*, July 13, 2006

McDonald, H., *UDA: Inside the Heart of Loyalist Terror*, Dublin 2004

McKay, S., *Bear in Mind These Dead*, Faber & Faber, London, 2008

McKay, S., *Northern Protestants: An Unsettled People*, Blackstaff Press, Belfast 2005

McKittrick, D. & McVea, D, *Making Sense of the Troubles: A History of the Northern Ireland Conflict*, Penguin, London 2012

McKittrick, D., Kelters, Feeney, B., Thornton C., & McVea, D., *Lost Lives: The Stories of the Men, Women and Children Who Died as a Result of the Northern Ireland Troubles*, Mainstream, Edinburgh 1999

McPhilemy, S., *The Committee: Political Assassination in Northern Ireland*, Robert Rinehart, New York 1998

Miller, D., *Don't Mention the War: Northern Ireland, Propaganda and the Media*, Pluto Press, London 1994

Moloney, E., *A Secret History of the IRA*, Penguin, London 2007

Mullan, D., *Eyewitness Bloody Sunday: The Truth*, Merlin, Belfast 1998

Murphy, D., *The Stalker Affair and the Press*, Routledge, London 1990

Murray, R., *The SAS in Ireland*, Mercier Press, Cork 1991

Myers, K., *Watching the Door: Drinking Up, Getting Down, and Cheating Death in 1970s Belfast*, Lilliput Press, Belfast 2006

National Archives, 'PREM 16/154: Defensive Brief D – Meeting between the Prime Minister and the Taoiseach, 5 April 1974 "Army Plain Clothes Patrols in Northern Ireland"' London; retrieved 31 January 2018

Nelson, S., *Ulster's Uncertain Defenders: Loyalists and the Northern Ireland Conflict*, Appletree Press, Belfast 1984

Nelson, S., *Ulster's Uncertain Defenders: Protestants Political, Paramilitary and Community Groups and the Northern Ireland Conflict*, Appletree Press, Belfast 1984

Ó Dochartaigh, N, *From Civil Rights to Armalites: Derry and the Birth of the Irish Troubles* (2nd edition), Palgrave Macmillan, London 2005

O'Brien, B., *The Long War: The IRA and Sinn Féin*, O'Brien Press, New York 1999

O'Callaghan, S., *The Informer: Life Story of One Man's War Against Terrorism*, London 1998

O'Leary, B., *The Politics of Antagonism: Understanding Northern Ireland*, Continuum, London 1993

Office of the Police Ombudsman for Northern Ireland, 'Report of the Police Ombudsman for Northern Ireland into a complaint made by the Devenny family on 20 April 2001', The Pat Finucane Centre, Belfast 2001

Orr, R., *RUC Spearhead: The RUC Reserve Force 1950–1970*, Redcoat Publishing, Chester 2013

Parker, J., *Death of a Hero: Captain Robert Nairac GC and the Undercover War in Northern Ireland*, Metro Books, London 1999

Punch, M. *Shoot to Kill: Police Accountability and Fatal Force*, The Policy Press, Bristol 2011

Rennie, J., *The Operators: On the Streets with Britain's Most Secret Service*, Pen & Sword, Barnsley 2004

Rolston, W. (ed.), *The Media and Northern Ireland*, Palgrave Macmillan, London 1991

_____, Drawing Support 2: Murals of War and Peace, Beyond the Pale, Belfast 1995

_____, Drawing Support 3: Murals and Transition in the North of Ireland, Beyond the Pale, Belfast 2003

_____, Drawing Support: Murals in the North of Ireland, Beyond the Pale, Belfast 1992

Ryder, C., A *Special Kind of Courage: 321 EOD Squadron – Battling the Bombers*, Methuen, London 2005

_____, *The RUC: A Force under Fire*, Methuen, London 1989

Sanders, A., 'Principles of Minimum Force and the Parachute Regiment in Northern Ireland, 1969–1972', published online May 4, 2016

Seymour, G., *The Journeyman Tailor*, Harvill, London 1992

Sharrock, D. & Davenport, M., *Man of War, Man of Peace: The Unauthorised Biography of Gerry Adams*, London 1998

Sluka, J., *Death Squad: The Anthropology of State Terror*, University of Pennsylvania Press, Philadelphia 1999

Stair na hÉireann/History of Ireland, Milltown Cemetery / www.facebook.com/search/top/?q=Stair%20na%20 hÉireann%2FHistory%20of%20Ireland%20milltown%20cemetery

Stevenson, J., *We Wrecked the Place: Contemplating an End to the Northern Irish Troubles*, The Free Press, New York 199

Sutton, M. (ed.), 'Sutton Index of Deaths 1969–2001; www.cain.ulst.ac.uk

Taylor, K. & Mumby, K., *The Poisoned Tree: The Untold Truth About the Police Conspiracy to Discredit John Stalker and Destroy Me*, Sidgwick & Jackson, London 1990

Taylor, P., *Brits: The War Against the IRA*, Bloomsbury, London 2001

_____, *Loyalists: War and Peace in Northern Ireland*, TV Books, London 1999

_____, *Stalker: The Search for Truth*, Faber & Faber, London 1987

Teague, M. 'Double Blind: The untold story of how British intelligence infiltrated and undermined the IRA', *The Atlantic* 2006

Tiernan, J., *The Dublin and Monaghan Bombings*, Eaton Publications, Hampton 2006

Toolis, K., *Rebel Hearts: Journeys within the IRA's Soul*, Picador, London 1995

Travers, S. & Fetherstonhaugh N., *The Miami Showband Massacre: A Survivor's Search for the Truth*, Hachette, Dublin 2008

Urban, M., *Big Boys' Rules: Secret Struggle Against the IRA*, Faber & Faber, London 1992

Urwin, M., *A State in Denial: The British Government and Loyalist Paramilitaries*, Mercier Press, Cork 2016

Weitzer, R., 'Policing a Divided Society: Obstacles to Normalization in Northern Ireland', *Social Problems* No. 33

Weitzer, R., *Policing Under Fire: Ethnic Conflict and Police-Community Relations in Northern Ireland*, State University of New York Press, New York 1995

Wharton, K., *Bullets, Bombs and Cups of Tea: Further Voices of the British Army in Northern Ireland 1969–98*, Helion & Co., Solihull 2009

Wharton, K., *Wasted Years, Wasted Lives, Volume 1: The British Army in Northern Ireland, 1975–1977*, Helion & Co., Solihull 2013

Williams, J., *The Rigger: Operating with the SAS*, Pen & Sword, Barnsley 2009

Williams, M., *Murder on the Rock: How the British Government Got Away with Murder*, Larkin, London 1989

Windlesham, Lord David & Rampton, Richard, QC, 'The Windlesham-Rampton Report on "Death on the Rock"', London 1989

Wood, I. S., *Crimes of Loyalty: A History of the UDA*, Edinburgh University Press, Edinburgh 2006

Woods, O., *Seeing is Believing? Murals in Derry*, Guildhall Press, Derry 1995

Index